FEARLESS HITTING

MORE THAN YOUR SWING

TIM McDONNELL

ISBN: 9798354607181

For God hath not given us the spirit of fear; but of power, and of love, and of a sound mind.

2 Timothy 1:7

The fear of the Lord is the beginning of wisdom: and knowledge of the Holy One is understanding.

Proverbs 9:10

There is no fear in love; but perfect love casteth out fear: because fear hath torment. He that feareth is not made perfect in love.

1 John 4:18

ACKNOWLEDGMENTS

My beautiful wife Jamie: In my first book a self published limited release, The Process, Becoming a College or Professional Baseball Prospect in 2003, I wrote that I wanted to thank the wife I haven't met yet. Well thank you Lord that has changed and I now have the best teammate I could've dreamed up. I adore you. Love U!

McDonnell's: Mom and pops have always been the best team mom and head coach for all of us. Our entire family loves and thanks you. Love you. Our team keeps getting bigger so love you all.

Sweet's: thank you for welcoming me into your (our) gigantic family. Love you all.

Charlie Reynoso: my non related big bro, thank you for everything you have done for Jamie and I and your support in this project. We are just getting started!!! The entire Reynoso family I love you all.

Michelle Clouser: new little sister for your constant support that I could get this done.

Craig Peterson: your guidance and help fitting me into your schedule so I could get your unreal gifts from God for design and help me get this finished. Always been family, brother for life and eternity.

Joe and Ryan Marcos: for your help with this book, your insight, wisdom and energy.

Shane Bowers and Teddy Silva: for answering my calls and texts with all my questions and helping with great ideas.

My college coaches: Howard Lowder (Chaffey College), Mike Gerakos (UC Irvine), George Horton & Rick Vanderhook (CSUF).

Coach Weathers: for giving me a chance to coach at Long Beach State, loved it and all my Dirtbags family.

My Indy ball family: Keith Lytle, Charlie Kerfeld, Mal Fichman, Jim Coffman, Butch Hughes, Buck Rogers and every asst coach and grinder baseball playing teammate I've ever had.

My original Marlin family: thank you Stan Meek for guiding, teaching and being Pastor Meek to all of us. Jim Fleming, Michael Hill, David Crowson, Orrin Freeman, Scott Goldby, Gabe Sandy, John ``Cheese" Hughes, Scott Stanley and RC (I'll get to you.) West coasters: we had it good fellas, way better than we knew at the time, miss you all.

RC: my brother Rob Corsaro, man you've been fighting with and for me for years, stories for days, so thankful we met and are still brothers to this day

TABLE OF CONTENTS

There comes a time for every player when they look around the clubhouse, dugout or across the field at the opponents and realize, YIKES! These guys are big, fast, strong, athletic, very skilled and extremely talented. There's nowhere to run and nowhere to hide. This is not a time to have fear, to survive and thrive you must be dedicated to finding every advantage.

You must know fear is your #1 enemy. Not fear of those other players but your own fear of failure: fear of being embarrassed, fear of making a mistake, fear of not succeeding, fear of disappointing family, friends or teammates, fear you aren't good enough or importantly for us today fear your swing isn't perfect. Fear my friends, is in your own mind and can be overcome by turning it into motivation.

Understand all of your favorite players, every Hall of Famer, MLB superstar, All-American and All-Star has failed. But they got back up, put failure behind them and decided they must out work, out think and out compete their competition.

Specifically for hitters, you must understand fearless hitting is not just your swing. Learning to hit is much more. There's no path or road ending in you becoming a perfect hitter.

Your hitting journey will be filled with heartbreaks, highlights and many daily challenges to overcome. You can do it. You can become a fearless hitter. I will do everything I can to help you in this book, but I'll miss things. You must commit to finding ways to become the best version of you. It's time to turn that new motivation into believing you can do it, never giving up, loving it, taking ownership and most importantly having fun on your journey! Let's get started.

CLUBHOUSE TALK

"WHY ME?"

Why write a hitting book when many already exist? Who are you? Good questions, I'll start with the second. I'm nobody in the overall baseball community. If I completely disappeared from the game only a few would care. Personally I think it's true for the majority of us working in the game, even with the high rate of giant egos. However, I still care about baseball, helping kids chase their dreams and hopefully guiding some through the bumps and bruises of their journey.

I was a decent player, had some feel to hit and played hard all the time. I don't say I played hard as a badge of courage. I had to play hard because I wasn't as talented as many around me. I envied the ease of Ken Griffey Jr. and others dominating the game without breaking a sweat. I was in the mold of Pete Rose, all out all the time. But, none of that matters to you and it shouldn't.

The gift I was given and want to share with others is gold. I've been extremely fortunate. I worked hard, was in the right place at the right time and paid attention to what some of the best players in the world were doing and saying. Some when they were teenagers long before they were household names and others during the peak of their MLB career.

I had the opportunity to be a college coach for future MLB All-Stars, Silver Sluggers, Rookies of the Year, Gold Glove winners and later scout and sign two MLB MVPs.

If you love hitting, imagine being a Marlins scout and standing around a cage in a major league stadium as Miguel Cabrera and others take batting practice and talk about hitting, pure and rare gold! How about being in a cage working with Giancarlo Stanton when he was seventeen? What do you think you could learn from spending almost every day with Evan Longoria for two years while coaching him in college? Talking with him about hitting, his swing and how to deal with the highs and lows of a long season. Finding drills to help Evan's development and watch it pay off at the highest level.

Do you ever wonder how the guys you watch on TV actually got there? You should. My goal is to give you some insight to develop your own game based on what I've learned from them or we learned together through trial and error. I'm not an expert. I didn't invent any of the things I'll share with you.

I'm thankful to the players and coaches I spent countless hours with over many years and just want to pass that information on. I honestly love 99.9% of the players and coaches I was lucky enough to be around. My hope is when they look back they say I helped them develop 1% of their total game. Some maybe more and I pray none say less.

"HIGHS, LOWS AND HEARTBREAKS"

I finished playing baseball at 29 and after two shoulder labrum surgeries, dislocated elbow, broken wrist, stress fracture in shin, partially torn hamstring, multiple ankle and muscle sprains and strains, bouts with plantar fasciitis my body was done playing. But my brain and heart still loved the game so it was into the coaching ranks I'd go.

I headed back to Cal State Fullerton and spent a year learning the basics of coaching from George Horton, Rick Vanderhook, Dave Serrano and Tim Wallach. Had the opportunity to watch pro players Reed Johnson and Aaron Rowand come back to train in the offseason and talk and learn from, both became very successful major league players. Coach Horton said I needed to dominate recruiting to have a career as a college baseball coach and the junior college level was great for learning so I reached out to another former coach.

I went to see John Altobelli who I had played for at UC Irvine and was the current Head Coach at Orange Coast College. I was on the last team when UCI decided to end their baseball program, sending "Alto" and myself to various schools. Years later UCI reinstated the baseball program.

Alto was a competitive fireball so it was a perfect fit and an environment I could really learn because he had already been a Division 1 coach. If his name sounds familiar then yes he's the legendary coach we lost in the heartbreaking tragedy we also lost John's wife Keri, one of his daughters Alyssa, along with Kobe Bryant, his daughter Gianna and many other special human beings. Horribly sad day for so many, they will never be forgotten. "Yay Yay" Love you and will always be here for you!

"LEARNING CURVES"

Alto and I had the privilege of coaching future major leaguer Donnie Murphy who had the self drive and mental toughness of a giant. JC players, that's how you do it, never stop believing, love the challenge, compete daily, out work everyone, never give in to adversity while continuing to battle and you will have a chance. It's a harder road but can be successfully taken. We had six players drafted in two recruiting classes with Murph being our lone big leaguer and many headed to four years schools across the nation.

It was then I headed to Long Beach State to continue coaching. It's rare and hard to keep going, but when a group of coaches decide to leave their egos at the door and do everything they can to develop their players, great things can happen. And it did, 14 of our players reached the major leagues and many more were drafted. It really was a development and learning wonderland.

Then I jumped into scouting for the Florida Marlins and in my first draft was able to sign six players with three of those making it to the major leagues. In fifteen years with the Marlins was able to sign eight future major league players. Two of those were 1st round picks, two in the 2nd, one 3rd, 2 in the 4th and one in the 5th round. I've been fortunate to watch and participate in the development of future major leaguers from a variety of angles and I thank all of those players for allowing me to be part of their journey.

"I THINK I CAN HELP"

The impetus for writing this book wasn't a single factor, rather many conversations and concerns from players, coaches, scouts and parents. Two major issues kept surfacing. First, many think the balance in our wonderful game of baseball is off and headed in the wrong direction.

Second and more bothersome is the rise of social media basement gurus and snake oil salesmen at every field feeding the fear and self doubts of players and parents. Trying to convince them they aren't getting the right information and only this special human has the answers they need, all for the low price of hundreds or thousands of dollars.

I thought I had enough information and facts I could actually help players and parents. Do I think this will be the best book ever written about hitting? NO CHANCE. I didn't play baseball because I thought I'd be better than Hank Aaron.

I'm positive this book will be just like me, full of passion to help players, parents and coaches, rough around the edges, unfiltered and imperfect. I do have three things I hope you get very familiar with.

I truly believe I can help any number of kids, if it's one or two or potentially many more great. I think I can do it. I love baseball, I love hitting and I love helping players develop and grow. Finally, I won't stop trying to help in any way I can. I'm not a trained writer, don't care what some may say and I pray God will use this book to help kids. Simple clear plan!

"FINDING BALANCE"

Baseball has always been a game seeking balance. Teams want balance between pitching, defense and offense. If one area is too weak you lose. Offense has many variables, one of which is hitting. Hitting in its simplest form is a balance of effort and accuracy swinging the bat. Swing to hard and miss, swing too soft and dribble it back to the pitcher.

Defense is about playing catch and being in the right place at the right time. Pitching is a combination of weapons and the ability to command and control the ball to throw quality strikes. Randy Johnson wouldn't be Hall of Fame member Randy Johnson if he didn't find a way to throw more strikes. When his walk rate fell below 4 walks per 9 innings he achieved a dominant status. Tracking his walk rate and dominance from the beginning until the end of his career is remarkable.

"FABLES SOLD AS REALITY?"

We are now in an era where hitters are striking out at all time highs. Fans are saying the games don't have enough action and many point to the movie and book *Moneyball* as kicking off this new movement. I don't know if that's true, but I can say the movie, while entertaining, also failed to focus on a few important facts.

I think the knowledge that shortstop Miguel Tejada was the league MVP and third baseman Eric Chavez had a terrific year garnering MVP votes himself were too important to not lead the story.

Their pitching staff had three dominant starters with Barry Zito receiving votes for MVP and winning the Cy

Young Award which is given to the best pitcher in the league. We can't forget the great seasons from starting pitchers Tim Hudson and Mark Mulder along with closer Billy Koch who also earned votes in the MVP race.

Four players in the top twenty for MVP is a pretty big fact to not get any play. But again I liked the movie. It was a "cute" story light on facts.

"METRICS"

We are in a period where analytics play a large role in our game and real life experience has been pushed to the side. Truth be told, I actually like some of the metrics. Many of the metrics are a refined way of evaluating results that may present a clearer picture of what happened. Not a bad thing, but metrics evaluate what "already happened".

The issue is somehow many have been convinced metrics are the sole key to development and can somehow predict the future. Metrics are here to save us, the players will get so much better and get hurt less. Well, the facts are not aligned with this theory and in dire need of balance.

We've pushed former major league players, experienced coaches and scouts out the door and welcomed kids with their computer that never actually played the game. Crazy! If you're a player and metrics are working for you then by all means keep doing it. Heck, Wade Boggs said he ate chicken every day. I'm not going to be the guy that takes away his chicken and makes him eat steak.

"LUCK"

Like I've said, the problem isn't the actual metrics. The wild predictions and false promises following are the real issue. Analytics people, yes I know you will say you make projections not predictions; you give possibilities not a forecast. Ok then why sell your information as fact and more accurate than the "projections" scouts and coaches have been making for years?

Do you need an escape hatch because you don't really believe what you're selling? You do realize many of us also went to college, right? We understand exactly what you are selling; we just don't see many facts. Theories and your opinion don't count. I could go on and on about algorithms and your "weighted statistics", but we won't be helping anyone.

Some analytics teams I'm positive are better than others, that's factual. But the bottom-line is this computer model says this while that model says that. Yet, did any predict, project, forecast or present the possibility of what Brandon Crawford or Salvador Perez would produce in 2021. Any metrics point to what Julio Urias would do in 2021? Very doubtful! I mean Crawford is 34 years old, I was told players peak around 27. Here come the supposed reasons or caveats, "well we are working on averages", "that is typical for players", "he had really good fortune", "he had poor fortune".

Wait. What? Did I hear you right, are you saying he had good luck? He got lucky this year? Yes, we're smart enough to know what "fortune" means. Now that's an enormous escape hatch. All these metrics, as we watch the game being changed and your answer comes down to luck?

Am I really supposed to believe Ted Williams, Lou Brock, and Bill Madlock, Dave Winfield, Tim Raines, Roberto Alomar, Jim Thome, Robin Yount, Chipper Jones and many others all very different hitters just never had bad luck? I'm just one guy already admitting I'm insignificant in the overall baseball community but when luck is the answer, we have lost balance!

"SUGAR, PIZZA AND SIDE EFFECTS"

Players have the best technology the industry has ever seen to analyze their game. The "gurus" are tracking every swing a young player takes in the cage. They have launch angle, exit velocity and distance for their "Cage Bombs", the indoor home run. They work for hours to increase those metrics but never learn how to hit. They watch their swing videos but aren't sure what they are looking at.

I'm not saying everyone using technology is bad, many are actually great but they're getting hard to find. Far too many just push the technology with little thought to the complete hitter, complete player and complete person.

We have kids training with the best science ever available but continue to drink an energy drink before and a "sports" drink after without realizing that's equal to eating 6 tablespoons of sugar. We have kids trying to use advanced metrics but never do a basic study on sugar. Come on, we have lost balance. We have teenager's weight training like they're in the NFL and follow with pizza or fast food for dinner and 5 hours of sleep. You guessed it, balance lost.

Obviously one of the main drivers for writing this book is we have kids being taught how to swing but have no idea how to hit. Balance is gone. It's heartbreaking and makes many angry as the game for kids is being destroyed.

I'm open to learning and maybe there's something out there I haven't seen. But it all feels like one of those commercials for some terrific medication solving all of our problems, but then they read the potential side effects quietly at the end. "This may cause nausea, nightmares and vivid dreams, severe blisters, diarrhea, unusual emotional dysfunction including anger and violence". Do people really take these?

I'm veering off the path for you young hitters, but I want you to see balance is needed. There's always unintended consequences that must be measured and evaluated. Don't get so lost in all the new and fancy gadgets you never build a solid foundation.

"GURU OR SKILLED SALESMEN"

Another big issue is those pushing fear and self-doubts to players and parents. They convince them they aren't getting the right information but this specially gifted human is here to save the day. Somehow down in their basement or "lab" they solely hold the key pieces of information guaranteeing future success.

We're in an environment where players have to fend off all the self-labeled "hitting gurus" in every corner of social media and the internet. Gurus show up out of nowhere and can't wait to attach their name to what a player has already done. Charlatans stealing money from people looking for help. Pathetic!

Showcase after showcase telling parents little Johnny has to be at this event to get the exposure needed to get a scholarship to their dream school. Travel ball teams try to convince anyone they can that your child must play for this "elite prospect" 10 and under organization or they will get left behind in the recruiting process. Oh ya and we do hold a tryout that you're going to have to pay to attend. Just stop it!

"THE GOOD, THE BAD AND THE GREAT"

Now before I get hundreds of angry emails, phone calls and texts. I'm aware of and I'm friends with many good hitting and travel coaches, showcase organizers, you name it but if those of us that have been in the game don't call out the imposters, fear mongers and salesmen we are no better than them.

So what should players and parents do? Check resumes, get references, second opinions, be skeptical and ask a million questions. Anyone with any value will have no problem answering any of the above. The good ones will help build a solid foundation that can't be shaken and help create or increase your love of the game while being both patient and positive. The great ones will make sure the player gets all the credit and it won't be because of this "special guru".

This is a critical and potentially career ending decision. I've heard more stories of players quitting baseball because of the amount of frustration and confusion some random "coach" caused than I can possibly count. Treat this time with the level of seriousness it deserves, do not wing it. Remember this one decision could be the last one you and your child make about playing baseball.

"DON'T BE A STEPPING STONE"

Knowing all of this, I've personally been hitting with a professional minor league player and stopped working with them to call a current major league player to confirm information or maybe get a new way of saying the same thing. For clarity, I don't charge players and I don't do lessons, but I will try to help a player if they ask.

We must remember we can't let confusion continue. Trust must be established, it's always about the player and his career. Never, I said NEVER is it about the coach. Believe me if you fail, most will forget about you and never mention your name again. For whatever reason, likely the amount of money they can make, these self-described gurus are everywhere and their goal is to be a famous hitting guru. They see players as stepping stones to get where they or the money can take them.

"TOUGH LOVE"

It's about this time when I hear, "OK Mac, we understand, we'll take this seriously, you keep telling us what not to do, but what can we actually do to become a better hitter?" AWESOME, it's time to have some fun and find out why so many of us speak about hitting with passion and love. Complete and total relentless obsession to help players find the same passion and love with the hopes they pass it on like many did for us.

Always remember baseball is supposed to be fun, but before we can go further I need to explain a few things and here comes the tough love. Having fun doesn't mean showing up your opponents, bats flips to the moon, yelling absurd meaningless sayings from the dugout, arguing with umpires, throwing equipment, foul language, bad attitude, lack of effort, acting like a tough guy or having a fancy dance move getting into the batter's box timed up with your walk-up song.

I'm good with letting the kid's play, but how about we play the actual game and compete with our team to win. This isn't some opportunity to get social media clout or a sweet "TikTok" video. When I say have fun and I will many times. I don't mean show zero respect for the game. The game of baseball owes you nothing and I promise it will teach you humility and it will be painful and soon if you keep acting like a fool.

Having fun is becoming part of a team, competing, getting mentally tough, having energy and passion for practice and games, working to improve all areas of your game, learning the details of baseball situations and getting better one day at a time.

The goal is to win games together; it's not about your personal stats or your ego. In twenty years people will care if you can be part of a team working together, no one will care if you hit .220 or .320, had epic exit velocity and launch angle, put the stats, the metrics, the nonsense behind you and go play for your team, compete!

"CAMI"

Former major leaguer Ken Caminiti, one of my favorite all time players, a man that played all out all the time, uniform dirty, grinding for every win, was asked by a reporter why he ran the bases so hard and fast after a home run. His answer: "I wanted to get back to my team".

I've told many players this story and I finally got to watch a college player in a game hit a home run, fly around the bases and wait to celebrate until he was back in the dugout with his team. Man, I was pumped to see that, he knows exactly who he is as I write this. Do you think I'm willing to fight for him in a draft room? You better believe it. Keep doing it youngster, others will follow and I will always fight for you!

"DRIVING FORCE"

So what can you do? Let's learn from some examples. Do you have a friend always doing some amazing feat as you're left standing there wondering how in the world did they do that? The hitter who doesn't overthink hitting or their swing, just walk up to the plate, compete and hit balls hard all over the field. The shortstop that constantly makes unbelievable plays on "bad hop" ground balls or the outfielder that always makes unreal diving catches.

Have you considered just for a minute this has very little to do with talent and everything to do with one simple truth. They thought they could do it, they were fearless.

Can it be this simple? Now I'm not going full motivational speaker here, but every great achievement was started with one simple clear thought. **I think I can do that.** Many actions follow behind, but the first thought cannot be forgotten because it's the driving force for action. Let's look at a few seemingly normal human beings doing almost superhuman feats.

"RUN FOREST, RUN"

Consider ultra marathoner Dean Karnazes. Among many displays of insane running, he actually ran 50 marathons in 50 states in 50 straight days. I'm not going to deny he may have some genetic gifts but a few things are very much true. One, he **thought he could** accomplish his feats. Two, he **loves** running. Finally he **never gives up.**

I watched part of one of his speaking videos a few years ago and he said, "you spend hundreds of hours training, you're dedicated to your goal, stay committed and sacrifice but time again you come up short but you never give up". He continued by ending with "I believe the difference between people who succeed and those that don't is not differences in talent, it's those who succeed are unwilling to give up no matter how dire the situation gets". WOW! Some great insight! Check out his website ultramarathonman.com, I don't know him but I'm willing to learn from great achievers.

"SPIDERMAN?"

Then there's Alain Robert, known as "the French Spiderman". He's a rock and urban climber but famous as a "free solo climber" which means he does all his climbs with no safety equipment, just a bag of chalk and climbing shoes. I heard about him because my nephews love rock climbing so I started searching videos and reading stories when I came across a man who free climbed the Empire State Building in New York.

The building is over a thousand feet high, is there any chance the entire time he was climbing he was thinking, "I hate this climbing stuff", "I'm scared I'll fail", "I don't think I can do this" or "I might quit half way up". No chance!

I'm not recommending anyone try this activity, he has been both arrested and injured. However, I do believe it's important to understand what drives people to accomplish these great feats. There's zero chance to achieve goals with self-doubt, fear, lack of love or any thoughts of giving up.

"ICEMAN?"

Wim Hof is a slightly controversial human, but there is no denying his accomplishments. Wim "The Iceman" Hof is known for his ability to withstand extreme temperatures. He holds records for feats such as being submerged for 112 minutes in an ice bath from the neck down. Wim climbed 22,000 feet of Mt. Everest wearing only shorts and shoes as well as completing a marathon in the Namib Desert without drinking water while temperatures rose to 104 degrees.

Why would any of this matter to you? Do you think he lives in a constant state of fear? No chance, in fact he claims anyone can do what he does with the power of controlling your breathing and mind. Do not attempt his methods on your own or without a doctor. However, a few things he constantly says are important to think about. One is anyone can do what he does. Meaning it doesn't take a superhuman to complete great accomplishments. Also meaning you can hit!

Wim claims learning to control your breathing you can get greater control of your mind, your thinking and emotions. He's telling you that you can control and eliminate fear. We actually see this played out watching major leaguers play big games. Learn to watch what is happening between pitches. Watch pitchers and hitters alike take depth breaths to slow their thinking and ultimately slow the game down in their head.

"THE LITTLE ENGINE THAT COULD"

Many of us grew up reading or watching films of the folktale, The Little Engine That Could. Do you remember the little train's signature phrase "I think I can, I think I can, I think I can". Somewhere along the line we start to doubt ourselves. Start working to change your stinking thinking and work on positive thoughts. You definitely can do more than you currently think you can.

However, I also know we can't allow ourselves to be filled with delusional thoughts and false confidence. There are basic talents, skills and athletic ability you need to play baseball and major league players are special in many ways. Work on being the best version of you. Be totally and completely honest with yourself about your own skills. When you know you are putting in the work then your confidence can be based in reality and not false hope. Start all of your hitting with the simple thought, "I think I can" and then get to work.

"STARTING BLOCKS TO BECOMING A FEARLESS HITTER"

1. Think you can.

2. Love it.

3. Never give up.

1ST INNING: A STRONG FOUNDATION

"HEY COACH"

Picture this, a player walks up "Coach, hey coach what's wrong with my swing? I'm really struggling". Likely the most appropriate answer if the player has had any level of success before is, "nothing, nothing is wrong with your swing". But you can't leave them there.

Literally every coach and hitting coach has had this happen and it's time to ask relevant questions. Now, hopefully the player is fortunate to have a coach that will go over the issues we'll discuss in this book or potentially a highly experienced coach that really knows the player as both a hitter and a person that can help make a very small adjustment to their swing if needed. Note the word small and realize small is of the utmost importance.

"STAY OUT OF THE SPIRAL"

HOWEVER, HOWEVER, HOWEVER, bells ringing, alarms blaring, lights flashing, flags thrown: what started as a very innocent question from a player to his coach has now become an extremely critical point in many baseball players careers. It's at this moment coaches want to help their players. I understand this desire. Young high energy coaches can feel the pain and frustration from the player and want to make it go away. It's why coaches began coaching, they want to help players.

So one change to the swing is made which leads to another change because the first change affected three other things and the spiral to failure has started. Do everything you can to stay out of this spiral to failure, believe me it has a bad ending. Here are some questions coaches should ask players before tinkering with swing mechanics and finding the spiral of failure.

I want to note, when you see a word in BOLD remember it, repeat it and know we will go through each of those specifically as we move forward.

"CAN YOU SEE?"

How is your **vision?** Are you seeing the ball clearly? Does the TV at home have the same clarity? In your classroom can you read the board from the back of the room? If you drive at night are the lights blurry?

It really might be this simple. We all sit and read computer screens, smart phones, tablets, play video games more than ever before. These activities can have a detrimental effect on our eyes. Eyes get fatigued, eyes change.

Short story, I was a catcher all the way through high school, but was playing a summer league game when I was a young high school player. As we know in summer leagues coaches move players around on defense for a multitude of reasons.

In this game my coach had me in leftfield. The game started and the sun was out, everything was good. As we moved later into the game, the lights for the stadium were on and the sky was black.

I could see the batter take a swing and heard the ball hit, but had no idea where the ball was. I stared into a blank sky as the center fielder yelled "IN". I felt lost and you guessed it, the ball landed about twenty feet in front of me. Routine fly ball turned into a double.

Did I need to "REDO" my outfield skills? Change the way I caught the ball, never play outfield again? No, I needed to see an eye doctor and get a prescription for contacts and glasses. Next time, same situation, see ball, catch ball, he's out. No overhaul needed.

F
EA
RLE
SSHI
TTERS
HAVEGOOD
_____

VISION

"CONTACT POINT"

We'll dig deeper into vision as we go but also know there is a connection between your eyes and your **contact points**. Let's get back to our struggling hitter and questions for him. From here on out we will call him *Johnny*. When you are struggling do you feel like you are reaching for the ball way out in front or are you getting jammed and fighting it off late?

It is very possible *Johnny* is either getting his swing started too early or too late. Again this would mean no swing overhaul is needed. Instead let's ask him what he's looking at to determine when he's starting his swing. Eyes take in the information and tell the brain what to do and the body responds. Hitters have to react to what they see.

You can give him a goal to hit one the other way if he's early. Go ahead and pull the ball if he's getting jammed. No talk about swing mechanics, something he can try to accomplish. Let the hitter react and create the movements to get it done.

SHANE AT SLO"

nple: I was coaching at Long Beach
ying an away game at Cal Poly San
going to use real names in all stories
ecause it's both funny and positive

We had a young player Shane Peterson, a left-hand hitting outfielder. I'd been watching him struggle for a few days and I knew Shane would never come and ask for help. Heck, Shane had a personal quota of about three and half words he'd use per day, just a quiet self determined and motivated kid. He was a mentally tough grinder that was going to work and work and work until he got out of his funk.

As I watched his at bats I could see his vision was fine, wasn't having any trouble making contact but the ball was getting deep on him. He would foul pitches off down the third-base line and muscle through balls fighting to get the ball back through the middle of the field.

During batting practice and his cage work he'd hit line drives gap to gap. His **approach** was good as he was trying to drive the ball in the middle of the field. I kept watching, knowing I had to be right. If I gave him information now there was a chance he could get internal, over think and then we'd be dealing with analysis paralysis. Analysis paralysis is when a player becomes overwhelmed with thinking about what they should do and they stop reacting to what they see.

Before the game started Shane walked by me and I said "How you doing pup?" Pup is a term of endearment used with the younger players, many coaches use it. The kids are like puppies, they grow so fast. Anyway, Shane responded right back with "awesome", looked me dead in the eyes and walked away. His body language was good, he looked confident as he went about his pregame work, no pouting, no "why me" and he carried himself like he was a hitter that was in a groove and "on fire".

Body language is very important, the way a player walks, posture and holding your head high speak loudly. Always remember your body language is telling a story to your coaches, scouts, teammates, opponents and fans. Don't let them see weakness, doubt or fear with bad body language. Shane looked good, spoke well and was showing zero fear because his **mental game** was strong.

As we moved into the game, Shane walked out to his on deck spot and it hit me. For clarity I'd never done this before and it will never work again. I went out and talked to him on deck and said, "Shane hit the ball over the scoreboard". The scoreboard was behind the right field wall. I remember him looking at me like I had completely lost my mind. "I'm serious. I don't care about anything else just hit it over the scoreboard."

To be honest I figured he'd be so early he might hit one right into the first base side dugout and hit one of us. But nope Shane unloaded and hit a long high fly ball to right field annnndddd GONE, Home Run. The dugout erupted, the pup crushed one. It was one of a grand total of two home runs he'd hit all year.

As the players cleared the dugout to meet Shane out front, our head coach Mike Weathers, "Wheaties", came over to me and said "Mac what'd you say to him?" Coach I told him to hit it over the scoreboard. "Come on Mac, no you didn't". We just laughed.

Shane gets back to the dugout and Wheaties talks with him and Shane tells him what I said and we all laugh. It spreads through the dugout and we all get a good laugh and our team has momentum.

As you look back through this story, what if tried to change his swing or talked about swing mechanics? Hopefully you're starting to see redoing his swing would've been a horrible idea. We obviously had worked on and talked about his swing mechanics many times in the fall and at various practices. His swing was not the issue. Just a very small adjustment he naturally made to start his swing earlier. His timing was perfect and off he went. Shane was

3-5 that night with a home run and 5 RBI's.

Shane continued on and ended the season with second highest batting average on the team at .328 and years later would play in the major leagues. I am so thankful I had coaches before me teaching patience and gave me the right tools.

I'm in no way claiming I had anything to do with Shane's career. But I can guarantee I didn't ruin it with over coaching. My hope again is there is about 1% of Shane's journey he would say I helped him.

"COACHES CORNER"

Here's a chance for you young coaches to learn, not from me but from Mike "Wheaties" Weathers. I'm not an expert and not qualified to rank coaches but I can tell you Coach Weathers is in the group of Southern California Legend Head Coaches that created the powerful programs in the west. Legendary coaches like George Horton, Cal State Fullerton, Dave Snow, Long Beach State, Augie Garrido, Cal State Fullerton, Gary Adams, UCLA, Mike Gillespie, USC and UC Irvine. Those were special coaches and special humans. Just ask their former players and they'll tell you.

So back to Wheaties, he had a tremendous sense of humor, extremely funny, don't get carried away though he ran a much disciplined program. But he and his team also had a ton of fun working to be great. The players loved Wheaties, they knew he had their back and truly loved them. Even when he was yelling at his players they knew he loved them. It was this reason his team fed off his energy, they really played off his emotions.

I can't remember exactly how many games later we were into the season after Shane's big home run. But, we were in a tense situation in a game and the players were tight, pressing and overall trying to do too much. Shane was coming up to hit, the negative feelings in the dugout were tangible and then I heard it.

Can't tell you exactly how he phrased it but it was something close to "Hey Mac, tell him to do it again, tell Shane to hit it out of here, LET'S GO!!!!" Instantly the team started laughing knowing it was a once in a lifetime moment for all of us, but Wheaties had a method to his madness. His goal wasn't for Shane to hit a miracle home run. He wanted his team to relax and have fun competing. It worked, Shane didn't homer but the team did rally and we ended up winning.

"COACHING 101"

Rule 1 for young coaches: you can be demanding of excellence, you can be the best mechanics coach in the world but if your players don't know with certainty you deeply care about them as people they will never fully trust you and your team will never really be "your" team. Instead it will just be a group of individuals with the same uniform. Love and trust take time. With honesty and patience it will happen but it can't be forced.

Quickly to you players, to become a team it takes everyone doing their part. Listen, communicate, be accountable, responsible and build trust and team love, it's so much more fun.

"BACK TO JOHNNY"

As we head back to helping *Johnny* I'm really hoping many of you saw the two new bold items and are starting to see our foundation coming together: **vision** + **contact points** + **approach** + **mental game**. All four areas are of extreme importance before we ever talk about swing mechanics or make any mechanical changes. So what exactly does approach mean? Many coaches will combine both mental and physical skills into approach and while they do work together we will keep them separated.

"APPROACH"

For simplicity we define approach as a hitter's attack plan versus a specific pitcher. We start with each individual hitter's strengths and then match those against the skills of whoever is currently pitching.

We classify pitchers in general categories and then add what they actually do that day. Many times relievers come out of the bullpen and we have to work quickly with little to no information so our categories can help us get our plan and be ready to attack fast.

In the major leagues and college baseball today they have tons of video and data on each pitcher. No matter what the data says we still must use our eyes and see what the pitcher is actually doing that day. Humans are still just human, we have great days, bad days and average days.

Baseball is still played by humans even though many want to treat them as machines, robots or a video game. Using our eyes will give us information we must learn to process and share fast.

"K.I.S.S"

As complex as many would like to make hitting, I continue to stick with the K.I.S.S philosophy (Keep It Simple Stupid) as the great Ted Williams said many moons ago "Get a good pitch to hit", still rings true today.

For example many of the most elite major league hitters will say 90% of the time they are looking for a fastball in a specific location. A pitch they consistently hit hard while also being able to also take advantage of a hanging breaking ball or change-up staying up in the zone without any regard to who's pitching.

It's imperative each individual hitter learns what pitches and locations they get their barrel to most effectively and easily to create consistent hard contact. Then they can build their approach from there.

Notice I haven't even mentioned the strike zone yet and there is a good reason. As a coach I have to be able to help every hitter and I refuse to box any of them in or limit their success. As with so many things I've learned in this game this too came from a player.

"STAN THE MAN"

We had a left-handed hitter, he didn't end up a professional but he was productive at his level, we'll call him Stan. Stan had a fairly long swing and as much as we worked it was still a very uphill path. He would literally destroy pitches ankle high and really anything from his knees down. None of these, literally none of these would be strikes in a traditional strike zone but Stan hammered those pitches.

Should I make him take those? No way!! Stan could generally handle pitches from around his waist down but had huge problems making contact up in the zone. So together we came up with his plan to attack anything down in the zone and take pitches waist high and above until he got two strikes.

Stan's eyes would light up when he'd read a scouting report of a pitcher and see "sinker/slider guy", "love it" he'd say. However, those days of high ¾ arm slot, hard throwers pitching up in the zone were definitely not his favorite. Did we just let Stan drown on those days? Nope, we had worked on his small ball skills and he became a pretty good drag bunter. We found a way to build a solid approach, just like we did with his two-strike approach which we will get into later.

All of our work paid off, he became a productive hitter in our line-up. Stan had good and bad days but overall we were able to maximize his at bats because his approach was tailor made for him.

For clarity I should point out Stan was a significant outlier. He was a very unique and rare hitter. I certainly want all hitters to understand the strike zone and attack strikes but I also won't get in a hitter's way of having success.

One of the key reason's Stan was able to execute his plan is because what he lacked in physical ability and athleticism he made up for in droves with his mental game. Stan was a beast mentally, totally fearless in the box, always positive, high energy yet as calm and relaxed in pressure situations as anyone I've ever coached. His self-talk was tremendous, routines great and the pitcher was going to have to beat Stan because he wasn't going to beat himself.

Hitters as you start to realize your vision helps create your contact points and both vision and contact points are keys to executing your approach. There is one big dark hole that can derail everything. The dark hole is your **mental game**.

"MENTAL GAME"

If your mental game is bad or nonexistent you will spend a lot of time in a dark and lonely hole. However, if you learn to train your mind and control your thoughts and emotions you may visit a dark hole but it will get shorter and shorter every time you defeat it. Bad self-talk like "I can't strike out" or constantly thinking about your mechanics as the pitcher is in his wind-up about to deliver the ball will derail your hitting.

Imagine for a second you are in a boxing match with Mike Tyson or a MMA contest with Anderson ``The Spider" Silva or whoever you think is a great fighter. All you're thinking about is throwing your uppercut, zero awareness of what your opponent is doing. I'm thinking you'll get knocked out in about three seconds, the same goes with hitting. If you want to be a fearless hitter you will need to be external and see what your opponent is doing, not stuck inside your own thoughts.

Let's quickly think back to the last section where a reliever is running out of the bullpen and we have to prepare our approach fast. Imagine trying to read a report of what he's done in the past versus using your eyes and timing his every warm-up pitch today. Which plan gives you more tangible information?

Players let your coach read the plan. Get your eyes on the pitcher. See everything he does. Trust your coach to alert you if there is world changing information. You must be external mentally and watch your opponent to get an advantage over them. Hitters have to react to what the pitcher is doing and must be external to do that.

I've dealt one on one with players thinking baseball was their only chance out of poverty, out of a bad neighborhood and their entire family was banking on them. Imagine the pressure a young kid can feel.

How do you perform under those conditions? Use tools in your mental game tool box to eliminate those, clear your head and play. It's not easy but it's also not up for debate. If you don't have tools in your mental game to find ways over, under, around or through obstacles you will not reach the ceiling of the best version of a baseball player you can be.

When your mind works against you, vision gets blurry, body gets stiffer, reactions are slower and you lose concentration. How in the world are you going to hit? Well you aren't. We're going to start helping you and eventually you'll have some mental game tools and skills. Then you'll keep adding more day after day and year after year.

"THE GOOD DOCTOR"

I'm not a specially trained mental game coach. However, I've spent many years learning from some. I will recommend some books from true experts in the resources section and we will dig deeper in our mental game section. But first I want to share this. On June 12, 2020 the world lost Dr. Ken Razizza. He was considered by many to be the godfather of sports psychology in the baseball world. At a minimum a leader in the sports psychology industry and seen by many of us to be a mental game Hall of Famer.

Ken worked with many college programs, specifically Cal State Fullerton and Long Beach State baseball among many other schools and sports. Ken also worked for major league baseball teams: the Angels, Tampa Bay and Cubs all had him on staff at some point. The players loved him. Doc Ravizza was an extremely unique and special man missed by many.

I was fortunate to actually take his classes as a player at Cal State Fullerton and then work with him when I coached at Long Beach State. I can 100% attest he had a huge impact on guys like Jered Weaver, Troy Tulowitzki, Evan Longoria and many other players that became major leaguers.

Superstars Justin Turner and Kris Bryant spoke openly about Ken's abilities to help players build their mental game. Use a search engine to find his books or check in resources section in the back of this book. Watch his videos online and start learning, dig in and enjoy. There are many options out there you can find and learn from.

"HITTING: THE ACT OF STRIKING ONE THING AGAINST ANOTHER"

We want to move our bat quickly to forcefully strike the ball, let's not complicate it. I've laid out a very simple formula so we can start building our foundation to become fearless hitters. Vision + contact point + approach + mental game and we have a basic understanding of each.

It's time to dig in and really understand why we need to address these and build a solid foundation before we start tinkering with our swing mechanics. We should certainly know all of these before letting some random guru completely redo our entire swing.

2ND INNING: VISION

If I had a dollar for every time I've started talking vision with hitters and they interrupt me to talk about how they see the ball out of the pitcher's hand, well I'd be a millionaire. My response has always been the same. Well congratulations, that's a good thing but you are extremely late to the game. Your vision doesn't start when the pitcher is letting go of the ball. In fact it should've started long ago when the starting pitcher was playing catch in the outfield.

"OK coach I get it, find out which player is the starting pitcher and then what am I looking for, like specifically?" Good question and the answer is everything, literally everything he does matters.

However, so I don't overwhelm you, let's set some goals. To be absolutely clear you must get your body and mind prepared to play so I'm not asking you to sit on a bucket and stare at him. Use your down time to take a few looks. Spend some time studying the pitcher instead of goofing off. We all know there is plenty of down time before a game, use it wisely.

Each field or stadium provides a variety of obstacles to watching the pitcher. Bullpens can be out in the open or completely hidden, do the best you can. A committed group of hitters can easily answer three fairly simple questions.

"PREGAME GOALS"

1.   What is the pitcher's arm slot? Is it a high ¾ or more- does his arm stay close to head? Is it more of a traditional ¾ arm slot? A lower ¾ arm slot which typically comes from sinker/ slider pitchers? Finally, is it a submarine pitcher? This information will help us classify him later.

2.   What is the tempo of his delivery? Does the pitcher work very fast through his wind-up or is it a slower more methodical delivery? I used to ask our hitters, if this pitcher was a DJ what kind of music is he playing? Punk rock fast paced? Rap? Country? Slow Jams? Pick whatever genre of music you think he's playing. We're going to need to work off his delivery tempo so it's imperative we know what he normally does. Of course a quick pitch is always an option for a pitcher but we are looking for the highest percentage of pitches.

3.   What kind of an athlete do we think he is today? Does he have a fast loose arm or a slow and stiff one? Can we bunt on him because he's big and slow? Are his feet quick? Can we steal bases on him because his body

moves slow?

Just start here and answer arm slot, delivery tempo and athleticism. Now think about all the other information you can gain to create an advantage to win today. We may be able to ambush him and put up a few runs in the first inning. When many teams are still trying to learn about the pitcher you already did. Here are some advantages we can possibly pick.

"PREGAME EXTRA CREDIT"

High effort pitcher is identified. He grunts every pitch. His head likely jerks violently, we call that "head whack". Arm recoils hard after releasing the ball are some examples. If made to work hard we can possibly knock him out of the game early. Make him throw strikes, field his position, focus on base runners, frustrate him when you can. Drain his energy and get into the bullpen early in the game.

There are times when a starting pitcher doesn't throw a breaking ball for a strike before the game. Play the percentages and hunt only fastballs, if he gets his feel for his breaking ball we will all know but until then don't be concerned. Obviously take advantage if one is just spinning or hanging.

Does he look injured? Why'd I ask earlier what kind of athlete he looks like today? Did we see him limp? Is his neck tight or back stiff? Are they trying to hide an injury and see if their pitcher can work through it? If we think we see something then we must make this guy work, make him throw strikes, get him off the mound (bunt for hits), fake steal, really steal, cause havoc and find out.

Did the pitcher scatter his fastball all over the place and struggle to throw strikes? We need to be patient and make him throw the pitches we want. Force the pitcher to throw multiple strikes. Really shrink your hitting zone and hunt for the exact pitch you want.

Don't let the pitcher off easy by chasing wild stuff. Let him walk you and the next hitter, eventually we will get a pitch in our hitter's hot zone and do some damage and score multiple runs early. Maybe he throws a ton of strikes so we should be very aggressive early. Get your eyes on him and pay attention to details.

There are so many variables and I could give example after example but if you don't put in the work and stay committed then none of this information will be gained.

What do you think the opposing team's pitching coach is doing during your batting practice? They are looking for small advantages, finding a way to get each hitter out and ultimately win the game.

All the old scouting reports and videos in the world are great, but don't forget players are human, not all days are the same. The further players are from the major leagues the more inconsistent they are. Find advantages.

"I SEE IT OUT OF HIS HAND"

After going through strategies to achieve our goals by using your vision, now it's time to get back to that million dollar answer, "coach I see the ball out of the pitcher's hand". Ok players tell me how? What are you looking at and when are you looking there?

The answers I've received have varied far and wide. Some younger kids say they are looking at the entire field and just pick up the ball when the pitcher lets go of it. While others make claims leading me to believe this player might have comparable visual skills to Superman.

I've always believed in letting each player be an individual including their vision plan, however there are limits. Without becoming overly complex and without the education or experience to pretend I'm equal to or evenly remotely in the same ballpark of a sports vision specialist.

Doctors like Bill Harrison, a well regarded expert every player should search for online and watch his videos. I don't know and have never met Dr. Harrison, only his stellar reputation so feel free to search for other sports vision specialists.

"EXPERIENCE BRINGS WISDOM"

I will instead let you know what I've learned from many coaches and players throughout the years. First let's have an understanding of the difference between a soft focus which is a fuzzier, slightly blurry type vision and fine focus which is sharp and clear.

As the pitcher is on the mound we have a softer focus (many like to start this soft focus on the pitcher's hat), as he goes through his windup we stay with a soft focus. Now combined with our soft focus and all of our study time we should be able to anticipate when his arm is starting to go forward. We should be able to picture a window frame where his arm is going to be. As we anticipate when his hand will enter the window we shift our eyes to the window and use our fine clear focus on the pitcher's hand.

Using this strategy even for the youngest of players they will be able to develop and improve both their anticipation and ability to have a fine clear view when the pitcher's arm and hand enter that window and release the ball. This is a very simple but exceedingly important strategy to build a foundation for all hitters.

After release we want to do the best job we can to track the ball all the way to the hitting zone and contact or if a ball into the catcher's glove. There are studies saying hitters don't actually see the point of contact of bat and ball and the ball actually disappears at some point. I would note it's why I often use the word anticipate and focus more on drills to improve all areas of hitters vision.

"UNANNOUNCED GUEST"

I had an incredible opportunity as a player. We had an unannounced guest at one of our batting practice sessions before a game, the great Pete Rose. I was playing independent league baseball and Pete was there to throw out the first pitch for the Chillicothe Paints in Chillicothe, Ohio. Who would've ever thought I'd get a chance to meet Pete Rose in small town Ohio at an Indy league game? No one, I still smile and laugh in some disbelief.

I loved Pete Rose as a player, his all out style, zero fear, aggressive pure love of the game. As for the negatives you won't find me venturing into that conversation. He was and still is one of my favorite MLB players. We were the visiting team and he decided to come out and talk to us and caught us all by surprise.

I will say when the MLB All-time hits leader wants to give hitting advice, it's the perfect time to close your mouth and open your ears. He talked about many subjects and we listened. The most relevant for us right now is he talked about really watching the ball and tracking it all the way to the catcher's glove. He told us he did it so much it became a natural habit to track the ball into the catcher's glove and his entire head would be turned toward the catcher. I encourage you to find some old videos of his at bats and you can literally see what I'm saying.

Needless to say I did my best to follow his advice and have always tried to teach this. For goodness sake Pete Rose had 4256 career major league hits. Since Pete retired from playing in 1986, Derek Jeter retired with 3465 hits and Paul Molitor had 3319 as the two closest. A few others are closer in total hits but their careers were over before Pete Rose finished. Albert Pujols currently is at 3301 and Miguel Cabrera has 2987. Will anyone ever catch him? I'm doubtful but would love to see someone try.

"CAN YOU SEE HIS FINGERS?"

Let's get back to our vision development and a few potential skills hitters will learn as they progress. Consider understanding when we see a pitcher's hand on the side of the ball it's likely a slider. When we see a pitcher's fingers point up to the sky as they release the ball it's a change-up. If you see the ball go up at release, only one pitch does that and it's a curveball. Many hitters talk about seeing a red dot on the ball as a slider is on the way to the plate. Some more advanced hitters say when a pitcher throws a four-seam fastball the ball looks darker, almost a brownish red color.

As hitters develop and learn to study pitchers they will start to recognize if a pitcher slows his arm down when he throws a change-up. Like everything in baseball there are many variables. However, start building your vision foundation and develop as you go, there are no shortcuts or cheat sheets, just enjoy your journey and get a little better every single day.

"GAME TIME"

It's game time!!! We love it, it's exciting and fun, but our work is not done. I hear people say baseball is boring. That makes me think they have no idea what's really going on. Let's learn.

"LEADING OFF"

Let's start with our leadoff hitter and their responsibilities. Every coach and every team has their offensive philosophy players need to execute. As for me I want my leadoff hitter to be one of our best disciplined hitters. I want them to be able to hunt for their pitch in a very specific small spot.

I'm not a fan of forcing the leadoff hitter to take pitches to try and see a bunch of pitches. I firmly believe that makes hitters defensive. I want our guys ready to step on the gas and go. Statistics and data throughout the years have varied some, but every study I've seen notes the team scoring first wins somewhere between 60-67% of the time.

I loved when our leadoff hitter hammered a line drive in the gap for a double on the first pitch of the game, right away we had momentum and they were on their heels.

We need our leadoff hitter to use his eyes and vision skills to shrink the area he's looking for. He must stay committed to get not just a good pitch to hit, but as our leadoff hitter I want them getting a pitch in their happy zone, period end of story. If they don't get a happy zone pitch then yes take it and force this pitcher to work as teammates continue to study the pitcher.

"DUGOUT"

From the first pitch to the last pitch every player in the dugout should either be studying the pitcher getting ready to face them or finding an advantage to win.

Many times I had our pitchers come up to me five to ten pitches into the game and say "I think I've got the pitcher picked". Meaning they found something the pitcher was doing to tip his pitches and unconsciously let the hitters know what's coming. We do need to show some patience and must confirm this information before we start letting all the hitters know. But, this information could be the difference between winning and losing.

Here are some things to look for that have actually happened. Some are quite obvious but many times it's a very small detail the pitcher doesn't even realize they're doing. There's no guarantee any of these will happen. But, when they do we want the information and we must take advantage of it. Throughout the years a high percentage of pitchers have something they do to tip their pitches and it's our goal to find out what it is.

Feet: Pitcher steps straight back in his rocker step and throws fastballs while stepping slightly back and to the side throws off speed pitches.

Ball in throwing hand: pitcher set-up his grips while getting sign from catcher and before hiding in glove. We can relay information from the coaching box or dugout. If the hitter can't see it we can use different verbal cues. Examples: "Hey Kid"= fastball "come on 22"= breaking ball. Remember to be a little creative because we don't want the pitcher to know we picked him.

Ball in glove: Both hands together just below face getting sign from catcher. Fastballs no change, off speed and glove will flare out, like their fingers are separating or pointing up. Small movements are typical here.

Ball in glove: Pitchers throwing arm hanging to his side as he gets the sign. On fastballs takes his hand straight to the glove and goes into delivery. Pitchers throwing arm hanging to his side as he gets the sign. On breaking balls quickly wipes his hand along pants to get better grip and likely has done so since he first learned to throw a breaking ball. A very hard habit to break and one I've seen many, many times. If you're also a pitcher, work on fixing this NOW.

Head: Pitcher gets the sign and never looks down before throwing the fastball but gets the sign looks in the glove and throws off speed pitches. Pitchers will do a variety of things with their head and we must study them to figure out if they are tipping their pitches.

Leg Lift: Pitchers lift leg in wind-up higher when throwing fastball than when throwing off speed pitches.

Glove: After the pitcher gets the sign and takes a split second break before going into delivery has the fingers of his glove pointing straight up at his face when throwing the fastball and fingers pointing more towards shoulder when using off speed.

That last one is a very small movement but I think you are getting the point. You must realize different pitchers may do the exact opposite of the examples I used above. Pay attention and learn.

I've said over and over baseball players are human. As humans we have many routines we don't realize we're doing and never think about. Everyone does something, we're all different but the only way we find out is if we use our vision.

Lest we forget we also need to pay attention to the catcher and middle infielders to see if they do anything different based on pitch type or location. Do they do it early enough for us to use that information?

There are many ways to help your team win and not even play. There is no reason to be bored or goofing around in the dugout. Stay involved, you never know when you will be called on to go in the game or pinch hit. Pay attention and be ready to go.

"CHEATING?"

Is this cheating? I've had people tell me they think picking pitchers or signs is cheating. The simple answer is no. It's certainly not illegal except when using any technology, electronic device, binoculars, etc. It must be done from the confines of the field which means nothing from the stands or watching a TV in the clubhouse although rumors of college teams doing this have been around for years. No buzzers, trash can banging or computer wizardry is allowed either.

I try to point out in other sports like football where it's similar to a linebacker recognizing something in a quarterback every time the offense calls a passing play. We often hear about defenses reading the quarterback's eyes or his body language, the same way baseball players are reading pitchers.

Quarterback's also read the defense, the QB goes behind the center and he's looking out at the defense, maybe he knows "the safety never looks at me when he blitzes", he learned from a scouting report, video or his own eyes because he's paying attention to details looking for advantages. The quarterback sees the safety never looks at him; QB calls an audible and throws one deep and touchdown.

In basketball if a player stuck his tongue out every time he took a shot but nothing when he passed, you'd be ready to block his shot. Point guard brings the ball up the court and holds up three fingers. They're going to run play number three, but the defensive team's players were paying attention on the bench or maybe in the pregame shoot around and they already came up with a plan to stop play three.

This happens in virtually every sport from baseball and softball to tennis, boxing, volleyball, water polo and on and on. There is etiquette to all of this but the general idea is if you are getting your pitches picked or your signs stolen, then fix it.

"IN THE HOLE"

Use this time to continue using your eyes and work on timing the pitcher. Get comfortable getting your stride foot down on time with pitchers' delivery and pitches. Focus hard on when the point of contact will be on his fastball. You want to work to be on time to make hard contact on the pitcher's fastball.

Start getting more focused on your approach, have positive self talk about what you are going to do. For example you might say to yourself get a fastball and hit it hard back through the middle. Keep these short and simple and use your own self-talk words.

"ON DECK"

Take some good practice swings as the pitcher delivers pitches. This is by far the closest and best look you have to see him. Visualize you are in the batter's box, use your vision, timing and take good practice swings. Think about where and when the point of contact will be, estimate it with your practice swing. You know your approach and are ready to go.

"AT BAT"

Your homework is done, time for some fun. Take ownership of the box. Get in your stance, keep breathing. Use your vision skills. Keep it simple, you know what you are looking for.

As Doc Ravizza would say, look out at the pitcher and say "bring it". Many hitters talk about this moment as being thoughtless, you've trained and prepared to react. Others just have a word or phrase they stick with to keep their mind clear. Many hum songs in their head to stay relaxed.

Find what works best for you. Don't try to be someone else, be the best version of you. It's your mind, own it, control it and master it and compete.

"AFTER FACING PITCHER"

Did you win the at bat? Maybe the pitcher just beat you, that's ok. However, if you gave the at bat away or beat yourself that is not good and can't keep happening. Whatever the outcome, you must learn and get better, especially the last option. Stop having a pity party and feeling sorry for yourself, learn from it, now is the time to toughen up and become fearless.

Be a good teammate. Communicate to and with teammates. Was his fastball sinking? Does it have good ride up in the zone? Is the breaking ball loose or tight? Does the pitcher get his hand on the outside of the ball when he throws a slider making it easier to see? Do the pitcher's fingers stick up in the air when he releases his change-up? Did he raise his arm slot to throw his curveball?

So many variables but we all need to communicate together. This is an area where winning teams consistently excel. Fight for every advantage your team can gain.

"PRACTICE"

Hopefully you are now convinced your vision is of the utmost importance. There is a connection between what we see and the speed our brain processes information. We will go through some specific drills.

However, you should know full books have been written about improving a hitter's vision, computer programs have been designed and websites dedicated to athletic visual improvements. If you want more information it's out there. Many of those programs cost hundreds or thousands of dollars.

I have great parents, the best and I love them dearly. They provided us with everything we needed. I didn't say everything we wanted, LOL. There is zero chance I would've gone to some special hitter vision training. Heck, I never had a single private lesson. What's even crazier is a very high percentage of the players I coached or scouted that played in the major leagues would say the same thing.

If a family has the financial ability to do everything, wonderful I hope it works great. My goal is and will always be to help anyone that wants it and to help as many players as I can to become the best baseball players they can be.

"VISION DRILLS"

As for drills there are many; using different colored balls, numbers on balls, coaches going through a windup and holding a different number of fingers at release, tinted contacts, talk of tunnels and funnels, balls on strings to the plate, training product lined up next to another training product. As you likely guessed there is huge money in this industry as well.

Many work, many don't, but it's impossible for another person to jump in your body and see what you are actually seeing. Try some that won't cost anything, see what works for you. Communicate with your coaches and let them know what problems you're having.

"EMPTY SEATS AT FENWAY"

My advice would be to start with the basics. The harsh reality is making it to professional baseball and especially the major league is remarkably, enormously and extremely rare and quite difficult. My personal opinion would be to limit spending big money until those are closer to reality than just a dream.

I'm not trying to be Debbie Downer or super negative. I'm just pointing out facts. From 1871 until present day (2021) there have been about 22,500 total players that have ever played a single major league game. Obviously each season more players get added to that number, but it's still a small number.

For comparison, Boston Red Sox Fenway Park has capacity around 37,000 seats, so if every player that ever played a major league baseball game was in a seat at the stadium it's only around 61% filled. Almost unbelievable but also true. Remember to love the game, have fun developing, but be realistic on spending big money. There are plenty of great vision drills that won't cost you anything to try, let's go over those.

"STICKS AND BOTTLE CAPS"

I've seen many videos out of the Dominican Republic of young players hitting bottle caps with broomsticks. This is a simple yet perfect example of vision training at its very best. Anyone and everyone can make it happen.

It's all the little drills combined that will help your eyes work quickly and help you be accurate with your barrel to make consistent hard contact. Broomsticks and small wiffle balls at the park, in the backyard, out in a field, on pavement, this can be done anywhere you like.

Many high school and college players do this with sunflower seeds. Get someone to throw them, see the release, track it and learn to use your hand-eye coordination to make contact.

"PEPPER AND A LITTLE FIRE"

I'm sure just the mention of playing pepper will get the "guru's" to put me in the old school category. "Why would you want to practice hitting balls on the ground?" I can hear it already. Well Einstein, likely because all the kids you're ruining can't make contact.

Kids, if you don't know what playing pepper is, it's time to look it up. Pepper helps hitters with their vision and bat control, two skills lacking in many young players today.

While these con artists are having kids dump and lose their barrel, fly open, load their "scap" which p.s. genius have you ever studied how the scapula moves? Why is it that many of your paying clients can't tell me if their "scap" is a muscle or a bone? Many of you are having hitters load their rear deltoid and you can't figure out why they all hook the ball, but go on and tell me how advanced you are.

Keep teaching that maximum effort head whack swing we're actually going to teach kids how to hit. Your time is coming to an end. You fooled many but now the proof or lack thereof of your theories is showing and the world can see your nonsense doesn't work.

I've tried being nice. I've even tried to help some of you but your arrogance and know it all attitude are tiring. I know you killed it in that semi pro Sunday league, but then had a career ending injury. I've heard it all. Is it that hard to admit you weren't good enough? Most of us have had to deal with that reality years ago.

It's ok to not make it to the big leagues because you weren't good enough, but your disrespect to guys that did is just pathetic. Just stop it. Let's actually start helping kids and put your fragile ego back in your pocket. Kids get back to playing pepper, I'm betting you will actually like it and get better at the same time.

"TWO EYES"

OK, quickly get in your stance, look at the pitcher and close your front eye, the one closest to the pitcher. Can you still see the pitcher? Do you need to turn your head just a bit to get both eyes on the pitcher? A simple, easy and free test done in seconds with guaranteed results.

We all can be certain using two eyes is much better than one. Don't believe me, use an eye patch and hit off a tee or do some soft toss. Trust me it's not easy. If God gave you two good eyes to use, then use them.

"WHAT'S ON YOUR HEAD?"

I know you look cooler with your hat on backwards or no hat at all, but how many game at bats do you have like that? Over and over I see the same things: hitters in cages, hitters on tees, hitters in batting practice, hitters everywhere yet they never practice with their actual helmet on.

Make your training game like and put your helmet on. Get used to the weight, the brim and ear flaps. Make sure you have a good visual path underneath that firm helmet brim. It's not necessary or possible to do this all the time, however you and your eyes will thank me if you add this into your practice routine.

"STAND IN"

I loved having my hitters "stand in" meaning they would stand in the box like they were hitting as our pitchers would throw their bullpens. This drill still happens all over the world but far too many teams don't take advantage of this great drill.

Coaches can have players verbally call out the pitch type or location as soon as the hitters are sure. Challenge the hitter to be faster and more precise or own your own career hitters and challenge yourself. We can even add a timing element to this drill.

Hitters in their stance, have good rhythm work on your stride, have good separation with your hands, get loaded up ready to swing but hold it and verbally say "hit". Use whatever term you want at your point of contact. Were you early? Were you late or right on time?

Have trouble versus left handed pitchers then "stand in" on as many lefties as possible. Communicate with your team's pitching coach and ask for a schedule. 99.5% of coaches will help you.

A few rules you MUST follow here or the pitching coach will ban you from his bullpen.

1. Wear a helmet for safety and to make it as game like as possible.

2. Remember you are a guest.

3. Your verbal cues should only be heard by your hitting coach, barely above a whisper. Use self-talk in your head if by yourself.

4. Only speak if spoken to and don't distract the catcher.

5. If the pitching coach asks you to "stand in" for a few pitches in the other batter box to help the pitcher. Do it, he doesn't care if you aren't a switch hitter. You are now being a good teammate and helping the pitcher.

6. After the pitcher is done with his bullpen shake

everyone's hand and thank them so you will be welcomed back again.

"PITCHING MACHINE TRACKING"

After a scout signs a player they will follow that player and his progress very closely. Always hoping the player is learning, developing, being a great teammate and ultimately will reach the ceiling you had projected. It doesn't happen on every player or every year but there are times a coach from player development will call you with either a really good or really bad update.

I received two of those calls in regards to Michael Giancarlo Stanton. Both good and this was the second, I'll get to the first later. However, being the second call I was less nervous when I answered Anthony Iopoce's call. Anthony was a coach and hitting coordinator with the Marlins and currently the major league hitting coach for the Chicago Cubs.

Anthony, a high energy very positive person called and had to tell me what the "big guy" Stanton had been doing. I'm paraphrasing here so forgive me but it was close to "Hey Mac I promise you the 'big guy' is figuring it out and he's going to be a major leaguer!" At the time Stanton was still in the minor leagues and he was somewhere between 18-19 years old. "Mac I'm telling you after every game he has us set up the pitching machine in the cage and just throw slider after slider, he's in there just learning spin and working on seeing the ball". "He'd probably stay in there all night if we let him. I knew you'd want to hear this so I had to tell you."

Awesome! Some exciting stuff. A very young man with loads of talent putting in tons of extra work to maximize his vision, that is called owning your own career and finding ways to get better.

"FOLLOW THE LEADERS"

I wouldn't even be able to approximately guess how many high school and college practices I've seen in the last twenty plus years. Let's just go with a lot. Many times I'll be near the batting cage and the machine is on just pitching easy fastballs right down the middle or hanging breaking balls with hitters taking monster swings and hammering the ball.

While there is a time for that, what I rarely see are hitters challenging themselves at practice. It's ok to fail in practice. It's ok to have the machine throw nasty sliders or curveballs or turn the velocity up and work on elevated fastballs. Learn to take pitches, learn what you can handle and develop your vision.

It was Giancarlo Stanton, not me, he showed you the way. Realize Stanton was a three sport athlete in high school and had very little baseball experience when we drafted and signed him in the 2nd round.

I literally had a veteran scout put his arm around me and say, "don't worry Mac, you'll learn, taking Stanton that high in the draft was crazy". Of course that scout said that after the "big guy" had his first year in pro ball when he hit .161 with 1 homerun.

However, we had done our homework and knew he was a worker, even better in real life than we had imagined. For clarity we weren't the only team that liked him but we took him before they could and we're not here to talk scouting. Anyway, Stanton only went out and hit .293 with 26 doubles, 39 home runs and just under 100 RBI's in his second season in professional baseball.

How? Stanton worked at it, he learned, he listened and asked questions. He had and I'm sure still has a relentless obsession with becoming the best baseball player he can be.

Young players please follow his example. Many players you watch on TV have similar stories. They haven't all dominated every level they played but they never stop working and never give up.

The credit for Stanton's career which includes an MVP award and multiple all-star game appearances all goes to him, he did it. He stayed after games and asked coaches to stick around. Worked on his weakness, maximized his vision, contact points, approach and mental game. Yes he had some help from people along the way but no one sprinkled "magic fairy dust" on him and turned him into a star, he did!

3RD INNING: CONTACT POINT or POINT OF CONTACT

You may be wondering why I wrote the same thing two different ways and I'm glad you did. When I was a young coach just starting to work with players I'd ask them how their timing was. In my mind I was asking them if they were in a good position to hit on time.

Very quickly I noticed timing was a loaded word having different meanings for each player. Many talked about timing in relation to different parts of their swing mechanics, understandably so. Others thought I was talking about the moment their bat hit the ball.

Timing is a word used in a variety of aspects in relation to baseball and I needed to be clearer and simpler. It was my mistake and I needed to change quickly. I adjusted to contact point and found it to be a specific moment in time all hitters could focus on without considering swing mechanics.

There are many times coaches and hitters have specific vocabulary words or phrases with specific meanings, we all have to be open to communicating and asking simple questions. Coach I think I know, but what exactly do you mean by timing? What exactly are you trying to tell me? There are many words and phrases in the game of baseball used in a variety of ways. Don't be afraid to ask for meaning or why. It's ok to admit when you don't understand or are confused.

When we discuss improving contact points we have to understand we are focusing on the exact moment our bat hits the ball and the results following. Our goal to hit head high line drives will guide the work we do when focused on contact points. I must use very general terms here with a full understanding that players come in multiple sizes and at a variety of levels of play.

When looking for your best contact point based on pitch location the best way to learn or practice this is hitting off a tee. A pitch right down the middle should generally be hit back through the middle of the field, think gap to gap at about head height. Inside pitch will be pulled more and outside pitch hit toward the opposite field, line drives at head height.

Start by working on the pitch right down the middle and focus on hitting line drives to the back of the cage. When struggling to achieve the goal, you must be open to moving the tee forward or backward. Do not move your body up in the box or change your swing for this drill.

Once you have achieved your goal. You can now move the pitch outside which will also dictate the tee will be moved back on the plate closer to the catcher or for inside pitches your contact point will be out further in front closer to the pitcher.

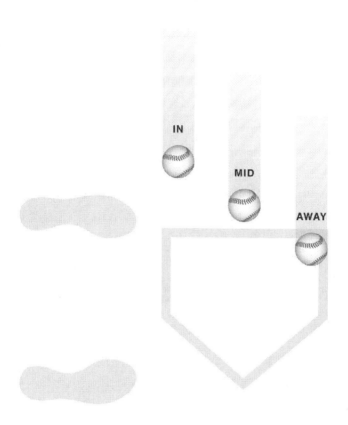

As you find your best points of contact, you can move into front toss and later batting practice. Remember *Johnny*, our struggling hitter, these drills are a perfect time to remind him to focus on his vision while getting his contact points corrected. In order to accomplish these drills the hitter must see the ball and recognize locations.

One drill to try in front toss is to have the player verbally call out location using "in, away, out, middle, mid" something short and quick, give them examples but let them use their own vocabulary. Letting them decide lets them use terms they use in their personal self talk they use in their brain.

As we work through this drill we are trying to get *Johnny* to recognize location with his eyes and use that information to reestablish muscle memory and his brain to body connection. We are trying to regain his ability to just compete in the games. To get back to automatic pilot to let for example the outside pitch get deeper in the zone before firing his swing.

I also really like doing this drill with young little league players. This is a great way to build a good foundation in hitting without confusing them with swing mechanics. You can soft toss a pitch and have them verbally tell you location as they hit it. Then ask where did you hit that ball? You called out the pitch was away but hit a ground ball toward the shortstop. Is that where you wanted to hit it? Why?

This small drill is great at creating an environment to increase their hitting IQ at a young age and opens up great dialogue. I've found through the years working on contact points and eliminating swing mechanics gives hitters a tangible goal without clouding their minds.

When a hitter gets to his good contact points and still needs some swing adjustments then a coach and player can talk that through. Personally, I've seen firsthand when hitters work out of slumps just by focusing on getting them back to their points of contact.

"LONG BEACH TO THE BIG A"

We were very fortunate to have Evan Longoria on our Long Beach State baseball team. Evan is a tremendous human being and as obvious to the world a terrific and elite baseball player.

His junior season he was under immense pressure as a potential very high 1st round pick in the MLB draft. We had scouts at practices, games and every workout we had. All of them were there to carefully scrutinize everything he did.

We obviously did talk swing mechanics at times, but I did all I could his junior season to limit those conversations. Even though Evan had a very strong mental game, I didn't want to be a distraction so when we did cage drills they were primarily goal oriented.

One of those drills Evan liked was having the person tossing squat or kneel back where the umpire would be in a game. The pitch actually comes in the opposite direction from a normal pitch. While accomplishing a few things, this drill gets hitters to make contact deeper in the strike zone. Hitters find out quickly if they wait too long to swing they will swing and miss because the ball is gone. I'd primarily feed him pitches in the outside part of the plate and he would focus on driving line drives to right center field.

Many years later, Evan was now a major league player for the Rays and they were playing in Anaheim versus the Angels. Evan generously invited me under the stadium during his pregame cage work with his major league hitting coach for the Rays. I told you he's a great human being.

Anyway, as I watched them do the exact drill we did in college imagine how happy I was to watch him execute his goals in near perfection.

I learned so many things from Evan that I've been able to use to help others through the years. Just watching him at times, taking in what he was doing and trying to accomplish. His teammates would do the same and then privately ask me to help them do what Evan was doing. If you get the chance to be around an elite player, take advantage and learn all you can.

4TH INNING: APPROACH

A few basic facts before we get started. Home plate is 17 inches wide, however the combination of the ball clipping the corner and the umpire's call on pitches it's usually much closer to 20 inches in amateur games.

Hitters need to learn what an umpire's strike zone actually is in each game. However, that should only come into play when we discuss a two strike approach. Until you have two strikes, all hitters should be on their attack plan.

Think back to what approach means: a hitter's attack plan versus a specific pitcher. First we identify the strengths and skills for each individual hitter and then match those against the current pitcher. Without diving into the endless supply of statistical breakdowns on pitch location and hitter's highest percentage of hard contact. We can identify the majority of batters hit the ball hardest in the middle 12-14 inches of the plate from around the belly button high down to their knees.

A solid and very simple approach for a majority of hitters is to dominate fastballs in the middle 12-14 inches of the plate while allowing them to take advantage of mistakes like hanging breaking balls or a floating change-up. Anticipating and hunting fastballs in the middle of the plate belly button high down to the knees and taking other pitches is a plan most players can execute with a high probability of success. I've personally had current and former major league hitters tell me that is exactly their plan 90% of their at bats.

The simpler and clearer we keep our approach the higher probability we will execute our approach. Always, remember we may have outliers like Stan we discussed earlier and they must be allowed to tailor make their approach.

We must always consider what kind of hitter we have. If

he's a power guy loving the ball up or a speedy left-handed hitter thriving on pitches down and away then let the hitter's strengths dictate his approach.

Some would argue to split the plate in half or to cover two-thirds of the plate. Personally I don't love splitting the plate in half unless the pitcher that day dictated it was necessary. This approach can lead to hitters taking many pitches in the middle of the plate and chasing off the edges.

Covering two-thirds of the plate is less controversial but also can lead to hitters attacking areas of the zone they don't handle well. If they cover the outer two-thirds they tend to make contact on pitches down and away on the edge that they don't hit hard.

In regards to the inner two-thirds younger players can have a hard time keeping pitches on the inside edge fair, we've all seen the very high and far home runs 20-30 or more feet foul which is nothing more than a loud strike.

When covering two-thirds of the plate hitters must be disciplined to not chase off the edges. Again, always let the individual hitter's strength dictate his approach while working off what the pitcher is actually doing. It's important to remember our goal. If it's to hit head high line drives or hit line drives through the outfield wall then the clearer and simpler our plan is the more likely we will execute and achieve our goal most often.

Don't give the pitcher too much credit and think he won't throw pitches right down the middle. Pitchers are human, exactly the same as the hitter and none of us are perfect.

"THE OVERSHIFT"

In the fall of 2004 at Long Beach State, Evan Longoria was our new recruit. We knew a lot about him before he arrived but we still had things to learn and quickly we did. Evan could pull just about any pitch our pitchers threw to him. Not a horrible skill to have, his bat speed was electric.

Unfortunately when he'd pull pitches on the outside part of the plate he'd hit many of those as ground balls to the shortstop. Hard hit balls for sure, but at the college Division 1 level those were outs. As we worked to refine his approach and slow the game down a bit in his mind, Coach Weathers came up with a plan.

He decided in our team practice intersquad (intrasquad for you grammar sticklers) games we would take every defensive player except the first baseman and shift them to the pull side of the second base bag. If he pulled the ball it was very likely he would make an out. If he hit the ball to the opposite field almost a guaranteed hit and our goal was to add to his skill set the ability to drive the ball to the opposite field.

There were times he'd struggle against it, but then it all clicked and Evan started hunting pitches he could hammer to the opposite field. Hammer is exactly what he did and until I saw Giancarlo Stanton hit balls I would've told you the hardest balls I've seen a young player hit were Evan's rockets to the right center field gap.

You might be saying well that's a nice story or wondering why we would torture one of our best players. The exact reason we wanted Evan to have that skill was all the data we had compiled on pitch location in college baseball was pointing to around 70% of pitches thrown in college baseball were pitched middle away. The data was significantly accurate with the colleges on the West Coast we would primarily be playing.

We did have to adjust when we played teams from the Midwest or East Coast, but had far fewer games versus those opponents. Moral of the story is to start working with players on their approach as soon as possible.

We had literally pounded our teams hitting approach of hunting fastballs middle away into their heads, but there were times we had to adjust mid game. I can vividly remember players saying Mac they are pounding me inside. Quickly we'd come up with a new plan. It could be as easy as backing up a little off the plate or to the hitters that could keep the inside pitch fair when pulled, then we'd just free them up to attack inside pitches.

Every possibility should be practiced. I love dominating the middle 12-14 inches, but at times we had to hunt middle away and sometimes we had to hunt middle in. I believe Coach Dave Snow is credited with the well known statement in the Long Beach State Dirtbags baseball family, "prepare to prepare, we are never set". Even though we had scouting reports on pitchers, even some video of previous games and created ways to classify pitchers, we were very aware we may have to adjust our pregame plan based on what was actually happening in our current game. I've mentioned classifying pitchers a couple times, now it's time we dig into it.

CLASSIFYING PITCHERS

Classifying pitchers is not some complex idea. Simply we are identifying a handful of keys to help our hitters anticipate what they will see that day and get their minds prepared. I have always liked these:

1. Type of pitcher.

2. Delivery tempo.

3. Arm slot.

4. Pitches and out pitch.

We also must keep our eyes alert to identify any unique characteristic (Ex's: will vary arm slot, pause in delivery at times, good pick-off move) or pertinent information our offense needs to pay attention to.

At the younger levels keep these as simple and basic as possible. As player's move on to the college and professional levels these scouting reports can become quite extensive. Please remember past information on players is more inconsistent the younger or more inexperienced the level of play.

Professional baseball has multiple levels, college baseball also has multiple levels, ages typically level out in high school, but each team's roster will dictate experience levels. Younger travel teams and leagues the player's performances will show the highest level of inconsistency.

Plan accordingly and don't overwhelm young or inexperienced players with information they aren't prepared to use. I continue to firmly believe the most useful information you can gather will be done in pregame and during the actual game.

"LISTEN TO THE INTERVIEWS"

Night after night, interview after interview we hear the best pitchers in the world say. "I just didn't have my curveball tonight" "my fastball was moving more than normal" "I tried a couple things but just couldn't find the strike zone tonight" "I just started cutting the ball more tonight" "Ya, I sort of made that pitch up in the bullpen before the game". It's quite amazing to hear but a good reminder that even MLB pitchers are human.

1. TYPE OF PITCHER

"CRAFTY LEFTY'S (AKA), A SOFT TOSSING LEFTY"

Many MLB pitchers' names start filling my head: Jamie Moyer, Tom Glavine, Mark Buehrle, Jason Vargas, Marco Gonzalez and Dallas Keuchel. When you read these pitchers' names, you should take some time to watch videos of them online. Start the process of learning how to study pitchers. The pitchers you face at lower levels won't be as talented but it will help you integrate all these approaches into your mind.

When watching these crafty lefties on TV or online, you will see this type of pitcher typically attacks a hitter away and possesses a pretty good change-up. As a coach you can discuss a good approach against this attack. Very often it is to hunt pitches middle away and really focus on driving the ball to the opposite field.

Another "old school" piece of advice is to move up in the box and closer to the plate. I often scratch my head wondering why most of the new generation either doesn't know this or isn't willing to try, but it works.

Every piece of pitch data tells us these guys pitch away or attack the outside part of the plate, rarely attacking inside. When facing a crafty lefty use one of the names above, maybe a pitcher on your team or in your league is similar. Instantly hitters can start anticipating their approach. It's an efficient way to cut through all the noise and get everyone on the same page quickly.

"Hey kids, we are facing a Jamie Moyer today" instantly they can start getting a visual image. Again, we aren't going to get an exact comparison but the other keys will help us complete the picture.

There aren't nearly as many left handed starting pitchers similar to Jamie Moyer these days in the major leagues but every level below the big leagues has many crafty lefties attacking hitters away, away, down, soft and away.

"POWER PITCHER"

Nolan Ryan, Randy Johnson, Max Scherzer, Walker Buehler and Gerrit Cole all fit this mold. Power arms attack hitters with fastballs. They will usually also have other pitches but their primary weapon is a powerful hard fastball. When this type of pitcher is younger they can struggle with their control and many times miss the strike zone with fastballs up and out of the strike zone.

A solid approach versus a power arm is to make them get the ball down in the zone and hunt fastball waist high and down in the middle 12-14 inches of the plate. Hitters, you can't help these guys by chasing fastballs up. It looks good, is difficult to stay off and worse hard to make solid contact.

And guess what, now you can actually move back in the box and back away from the plate. Commit to keeping your eyes down in the zone, ready to attack a fastball from the waist and down. If he throws anything above, just take until two strikes.

If you are a young player and you hear. "We are facing a Gerrit Cole today", don't freak out and run home thinking you can't get a hit against Gerrit Cole. Trust me Gerrit won't be pitching against you today. Just remember, Gerrit Cole, ok coach, I'll hunt fastballs from my waist down in the middle 12-14 inches of the plate and battle if I get two strikes. Perfect!

"FINESSE ARTIST"

Greg Maddux, Madison Bumgarner, Felix Hernandez, Lance Lynn, Max Fried, Shane Bieber. I just named some of the best pitchers to ever live, don't panic. These pitchers cover a wide spectrum of individual pitchers. So let's focus on what they have in common.

First, they use at least three different pitches, many times more. None of those pitches is extremely better than the others which can mean a few pitches are really good or all of his pitches are below average. They mix those pitches in different counts, changing speeds and executing locations. Most importantly they have good control. They throw a lot of strikes and likely will not walk many hitters today.

Our other keys are going to be important to identify these guys, but what is our approach? In general, those of you reading this right now are not likely to be facing Shane Bieber in a game soon. We're not going to give these guys too much credit and think they won't make mistakes.

As a matter of fact, I had the privilege of scouting Shane in college at UC Santa Barbara. Shane had great control but I saw him a number of days where the hitters hit him pretty good and he had his struggles. Important for young players to remember the guys you see on TV once were your age. They went through the same growing pains as you. The difference is they just refused to stop developing.

Back to our approach versus a finesse artist, my personal favorite is to hunt in the middle 12-14 inches of the plate and look to drive the ball from gap to gap. Keep it simple and know the pitcher is human and will make mistakes in the middle of the plate.

Some may choose to cover the outer or inner two-thirds but here comes the warning! These pitchers are looking to get you to swing just off the edges of the plate or on the black area of the plate which are much harder to consistently hit hard. If you choose the two-thirds approach you must stay extremely disciplined.

"SINKER-SLIDER"

Derek Lowe, Tim Hudson, Mike Leake, Corey Kluber, Sandy Alcantara and Lance McCullers Jr. at times fit this classification. This type of starting pitcher in the major leagues is another extremely rare breed. MLB has really turned to starting pitchers with four seam fastballs pitching up in the strike zone. However, many hard throwing relievers are dominating with their sinker. We will get to those relievers later.

However, college baseball and lower levels will still see this type of attack from a starting pitcher. The sinker-slider pitcher will attack the bottom of the strike zone with the intent that hitters will pound the ball into the ground for easy outs.

They aren't looking to pile up big strikeout numbers. Actually many would prefer you swing at the first pitch and hit a ground ball to an infielder. This allows them to keep their pitch count down and pitch deeper into the game.

If you're wondering if these guys have a third pitch like a change-up, the answer is yes. They may have any number of various pitches, a split fingered fastball, maybe even a curveball similar to McCullers Jr. The bottom line is they will typically attack the bottom of the zone. Once again hitters can make a box adjustment. You can move up in the box and hit the sinker before it fully sinks or move back in the box and force the pitcher to get the ball up more than they normally like to.

Our approach versus sinkers is always to make them get the ball up and our intent is to hit line drives all over the field. You will need to show patience because many of these guys won't give in easily, that's the battle. Take your walks if needed. Force him to do things he doesn't want to do. Grind out your at bats and win one pitch at a time.

The above four categories will give you a solid foundation to build your approach. But, we must consider a few rarer type pitchers.

"ONE DOMINANT"

If you're from my generation immediately you'd think Mariano Rivera and his cutter or Trevor Hoffman and his nasty change-up. If you are younger, picture Aroldis Chapman and his 100 mph fastball or Zach Britton and his power sinking fastball. Again, unless you're playing on TV it's likely you won't see any pitch as dominant, but you have the idea in your head.

What you will see is a pitcher throwing his best pitch 60% or more of the time. Mariano had a straight fastball, but rarely used it, Chapman has his slider. However, we must get focused on that one dominant pitch, know they will use it and attack hitters with it.

We will approach them knowing what to anticipate and making sure we hunt for it in the strike zone. Hitters must be disciplined against these pitchers. Commit to hunt in locations you can handle and attack that zone. Many of these at bats can become a two strike count situation. However, you have your two strike approach, so save the battle until then.

Many college relievers will come in and pound hitters with sliders. You're prepared, hunt for slider strikes in the middle 12-14 inches of the plate. Yes these pitchers typically have one very good pitch, but the fact remains you are playing on the same field as them.

Do NOT overestimate how good they are or the pitch is. They are human just like you. It's time to use your vision, have a good approach, keep a positive attack mentality, trust yourself and you can succeed.

"SUBMARINE"

Once again many names start flooding our heads depending on your age. Gene Garber, Dan Quisenberry, Kent Tekulve, Chad Bradford, Brad Zieler, Byung-Hyun Kim, Darren O'Day and today the Giants Tyler Rogers.

They have the big bend at the waist, awkwardly swinging their arm back behind them and then releasing the ball from somewhere below the waist to just off the dirt making for some tough at bats. Submariners need movement and pinpoint control to thrive.

The sinking fastball, the big sweeping slider appearing to rise and a change-up dying on arrival to the plate can be beat. You will need patience and strong discipline to wait for and then jump on a mistake.

Hitters want to make these pitchers get the ball up in the zone to succeed. Chasing down at the knees and below is often seen. Stay relaxed and force them to work and make that fatal pitch up above your knees and in the middle of the plate and line the ball right back through the middle of the field.

"WATCH THE LANDING"

A tip: we talked about picking pitchers and many submarine type pitchers have a common tell in their delivery. It's not always easy to see. But here it is; when their stride foot lands straight at the hitter it's often a slider and when their stride foot swings out to the side even just a few inches it's often a fastball or change-up.

I've seen a high percentage of submariners do this. I've even watched submariners at the major league level do it. Your job again is to watch when they are warming up and facing all the hitters before you to see if it's there.

The trick to using this is being able to quickly shift your eyes from the foot landing and into the window frame as they are releasing the ball. This gives you the ability to track the ball as your brain is telling you if it's the slider or either fastball-change-up. I did say it's not easy but it is achievable.

Once again you must practice this skill. Get with a friend, use wiffle balls to train your eyes to shift from the stride foot landing and into the window frame. Teach your brain to process the information as you are tracking the pitch to the plate.

"KNUCKLEBALLER"

Phil and Joe Niekro, Charlie Hough, Tim Wakefield, R.A. Dickey gave hitters nightmares. As a young player you may go months, maybe years and it's even possible you will never face a really good knuckleballer. Be thankful because when they are good you might as well take a tennis racket to home plate.

Hitters often swing where they thought the ball was and then it's gone. Saying these guys are rare is probably an understatement. I have very little actual real life experience against a true knuckleballer. The fact is I only faced one pitcher that made his main feature a real knuckleball. I can't say I had any success.

For this type of pitcher I'll let you design your own approach. If and I do mean if you figure it out then let the rest of the world know. I would say in reality most of the pitchers trying to develop this pitch aren't successful. If you face a knuckleballer just be patient and wait for a knuckle that doesn't knuckle. Instead it will flatly float to the plate.

The key here is to stay under control and focus on head high hard line drives. You may be tempted to try and destroy it which will likely lead to you rolling over and hitting a weak ground ball or popping the ball straight up for a routine out.

2. DELIVERY TEMPO

The pitcher is the DJ. Can you hear the music? What's the DJ playing? This should never turn into a long activity. Hitters should be able to identify delivery tempo rather quickly. We're looking for something unusual. An extremely up tempo and fast delivery, a slower more methodical delivery, a pause in the delivery, however many fall into some form of a traditional delivery tempo.

As a coach this is a good way to start a conversation and remind players to watch the pitcher. Start building their vision and rhythm with the added benefit for a quick mentality check in. This can get players to relax and have a little pregame fun, but don't allow this to turn into a goof off session.

Players this should be most important to you. Hitters must learn to dance with the pitcher. He tells you when you are starting your swing. His delivery tempo gives you an idea how to anticipate his arm and hand coming into the all important window frame. The pitcher controls the tempo and you react to it. Take the time to implement this into a daily habit.

3. ARM SLOT

Coach, I'm a hitter. Why do I care about the pitcher's arm slot? First and most important we are going to create a habit forcing you to find the precious window frame where the pitcher will release the ball. Second, this will give us a general idea how the pitcher may attack hitters. Finally this will help us determine the potential movement of his pitches.

Determining the pitcher's arm slot and what that means should be done quickly. Helping us evaluate the pitcher and come up with our attack plan. In order to define arm slots I've always liked using the way it was described to me.

A submarine pitcher is essentially releasing the ball below their waist to just off the ground, sidearm is from a pitcher's side or half the way up, three quarters arm slot would refer to ¾ of the way up from the ground until reaching the overhead slot in which the arm travels and ball is released almost over the pitcher's head. It's important to remember there are exceptions to every rule, use these as guidelines.

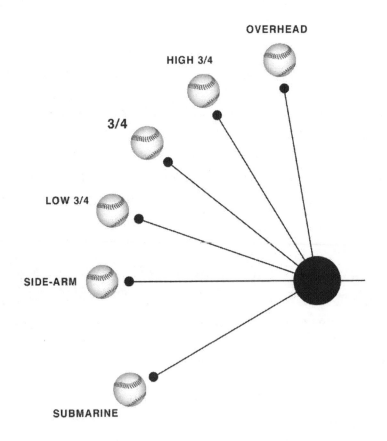

"Overhead = (OH), also referred to as over the top (OTT)"

These arm slots typically attack hitters using a north and south or up and down approach. Their goal is to move the hitter's eyes up and down in the zone. They routinely use their fastball or curveball at the top of the zone and above and follow with pitches down in the zone and below, like a downward breaking curveball.

Their pitches will have little to no side action and often will be described as having a straight fastball. As stated above they frequently have a curveball with 12 to 6 break and can have a split-finger fastball or change-up, but it will be very difficult to throw a slider from this slot.

Examples: Mark Melancon, Sandy Koufax, Ron Guidry are very close, could be listed as very H ¾ but, former Red Sox Hideki Okajima stands out as a true over the top pitcher.

"High Three Quarters = H ¾, (HTQ)"

A very conventional slot used by many due to the health and longevity benefits while also giving the pitcher the ability to throw any pitch they want. Many such as current Dodger Walker Buehler focus on a north and south attack. Hitters must know virtually any weapon is possible. Although a slider or two seam sinking fastball are rare if the pitcher does have one they tend to be an effective weapon for them.

Examples: Nolan Ryan, Dwight Gooden, Trevor Hoffman, Walker Buehler, Yu Darvish.

"Three Quarters = ¾ (TQ)"

True ¾ is a traditional arm slot commonly seen at all levels. Comparable to H ¾ this slot allows for all weapons to be executed. The pitchers can attack north and south but hitters will start to see many more executing east to west or a side to side attack. These pitchers will work more on and off the edges of the plate trying to get hitters to expand the strike zone.

Hitters will regularly see more sinking fastballs from these pitchers than the H ¾ slot but cannot eliminate any options. Hitters must move quickly to what type of pitcher, delivery tempo, using vision and communicating with teammates to put together a solid approach.

Examples: Bob Gibson, Curt Schilling, Fernando Valenzuela, Pedro Martinez, Jacob DeGrom.

"Low Three Quarters = L ¾ (LTQ)"

A low three quarters slot pitcher will primarily attack east to west or side to side, this does not mean they won't pitch up and down in the strike zone, but the action to their pitches work more side to side.

This arm slot would lend itself to two seam or sinking fastballs that also can have run (side action), sliders and change-ups. Terrifically difficult, nearing impossible to throw curveballs, cutters or split finger fastballs from this arm slot. If they do have these pitches, look for them to vary their arm slot.

Examples: Randy Johnson, Dennis Eckersley, Goose Gossage, Trevor Rogers, Tommy John (yes, he's known for more than just surgeries named after him).

"Sidearm = (SA)"

Sidearm versus low three quarters is a level of hair splitting I honestly don't do. At both angles the attack capabilities are virtually the same. The one note I'd make is the lower the arm slot goes it eliminates the ability to throw a curveball and increases the width of sliders.

As you have likely noticed I've been using a variety of major league pitchers names with the hope you will search for their video and watch arm slots, delivery tempo, attack methods, pitches and out pitch.

You decide would you list the following pitchers in sidearm or low three quarters? Maybe you think one or more should be in the submarine category. Feel free to do so, it's your career and you must learn to own it.

Examples? Chris Sale, Steve Cisheck, Pat Neshek, Justin Masterson

"Submarine = (SUB)"

I've already gone over submariners above in type of pitcher, refer back but start watching some video. Increase your baseball history knowledge and most critically baseball IQ.

One final piece of essential information is to realize pitchers often have a wandering arm slot. A wandering arm slot means this pitcher may use multiple slots either for deception or do so unknowingly.

Keep your eyes and brain active, it's possible a true ¾ arm slot pitcher will raise his arm slot to throw curveballs. They may literally tip hitters with where their arm slot is on any pitch, keep watching and paying attention, stay locked in and focused mentally.

4. PITCHES AND OUT PITCH

Pregame scouting reports are based on what the pitcher did in the past. Typically teams will have notes on type of pitches, which likely include velocity. The notes might include any specific movement of each pitch and in bold would indicate his out pitch. Out pitch is the one he'd use when he wanted a strikeout or needed to make a big pitch.

Again, please be smart and remember every level lower than the major leagues the players are less consistent and oftentimes are working on developing a new pitch, changing their delivery and always trying to find ways to get better. Hitters and teams must always be expecting a possible change or new weapon, don't assume the pitcher hasn't made a change.

As a scout I can vividly remember two recent Division 1 college pitchers that made significant changes during the season, both were good players. One was in his third year in college; I'd literally watched him start about 15 times over three seasons. As I sat at this game I noticed when he had two strikes on hitters he was now using a hard slider I'd never seen before.

I called him that night just to make sure I wasn't going crazy. He confirmed the slider was brand new and he had developed it because he was having trouble putting hitters away with two strikes. He finished his 6 inning outing with nine strikeouts and his opponents had no idea it was coming.

The second was a pitcher I had also seen through his high school career, he'd always been an up tempo, high effort, H ¾ slot pitcher that focused on his 4 seam fastball, curveball and change-up. In fall ball he basically looked the same but over winter break did a complete redo to everything and started the season with a slower methodical delivery, a lowered true ¾ slot while focusing on throwing 2 seam sinking fastballs, a brand new slider and a change-up. He had one good start, two very bad and then reverted all the way back. FYI: he also ended up with a sore shoulder.

Hitters and teams relying solely on scouting reports were not "prepared to prepare" for a quick change to their approach. Use your vision to see what the pitcher is actually doing today. The day you face him is what matters, communicate with coaches and teammates and continue throughout the entire game.

5TH INNING: MENTAL GAME

Many PhD researchers, psychologists, mental performance coaches, mindset experts, Navy Seals or Special Forces and on and on have written very insightful mental skills books. I encourage you to read as many as possible and get a variety of opinions, methods, vocabulary and skills.

Take a dive into learning visualization techniques, visualization is a mental exercise to see or practice yourself being a successful performer in your mind. Close your eyes and create the movie of you performing in tough situations, battling to win a two strike at bat or anything you want to work on. Players with injuries that physically can't practice should be taking advantage of these exercises, but in reality all players should learn how to implement visualization exercises.

However, what I'm going to do is bring you with me. I want you to see what I saw from the front row as I was coaching and scouting some of the best baseball players in the world. What I learned from them are skills you can start applying to your daily routines, practices and games to become fearless mentally.

The truth is for many of you it will be necessary "to fake it, until you make it". What does that mean? First, simply start believing you can do it. Then take actions while you are in the process of acquiring and finally mastering your mental skills and mental game.

There is no magic button, no app, no computer program, you will need to put in the work and earn these. I promise you will have failures and setbacks, keep adjusting, keep learning and making changes and as long as you don't quit you will improve your mental game.

"DUGOUT VIEW"

JERED WEAVER

Jered was entering his junior year when I joined the coaching staff at Long Beach State. I had no impact on coaching him or any of our pitchers. That was Troy Buckley's job and he was dominating doing it.

However, I was able to daily interact and watch Jered's progress. From day one I could tell you he was hilarious, always had an ability to make people laugh and relax, but he also had a skill I had seen before but never at this level.

Jered was able to shift from joking in one moment and instantly get locked in and focused on his work in the next moment. He was 100% able to be focused and completely present in each and every moment. I'd see this in his catch play and his bullpens when he would own and execute every single throw with an absolute purpose. His attention to each detail was impressive. His bullpens were surgical, get sign, deep breath, let it out and execute over and over again with precision. He did the same versus our own hitters at practice and then the season started.

Blair field, the home stadium for Long Beach State Dirtbags Baseball was packed. Opening day was here and Jered Weaver was on the mound. Fans, scouts, media, people were everywhere.

Jered proceeded to strike out the first ten USC Trojan hitters coming to the plate. An almost unbelievable feat he would later repeat versus the BYU Cougars as well as a 16 strikeout performance at Wichita State and 17 punch-outs versus University of Pacific. Jered ended the season 15-1 with a 1.63 ERA and in 144 innings piled up 213 strikeouts against only 21 walks. Almost every stadium would announce record setting attendance on the nights he'd pitch but none of that is what you really need to know.

What is important for you is every single pitch looked the same: sign, breath and execute, sign, breath and execute over and over again. He might get the ball back from the catcher and look out in the outfield or fix his hat after a ball call or a pitch he didn't like. He might clean off the rubber with his cleats but as soon as he looked in at the catcher it was sign, breath and execution.

Obviously he would go on and do great things in major league baseball with the Angels, winning 20 games in a season, pitching a no-hitter, winning 150 games and striking out more than 1600 hitters in his career.

Fortunately for us here in Southern California we were able to watch him frequently and for me I just wanted to watch one thing: sign, breath and execute and see if he continued using it and the answer was yes, but it became less obvious to the eye. There were times his breaths were bigger or deeper but as he matured he had more control over it and looked to use it when he needed it. Being in the present moment and owning each moment is of supreme importance.

So how do you create the ability to be completely focused, immersed in and concentrate on a task without getting distracted before completing or winning the moment? Start small: win brushing your teeth, making your bed, win taking out the trash, then add in winning in the classroom, win in the weight room, win being the first to practice or last to leave, win sweeping the dugout, win communicating with teachers, parents, coaches and friends.

As a hitter it starts with one baseball on a tee, learn to get focused on one swing. When moving on to soft toss, slow your practice sessions down. The game of baseball is played one pitch at a time, win each pitch. Rapid fire swings with zero thought have very little value other than loosening up your body. One good swing has more value than a hundred thoughtless.

Jered was the first MLB star I was able to watch before and after and I'm really glad I paid attention and luckily for me I'd get to see it again.

TIM MCDONNELL

TROY TULOWITZKI "TULO"

I had the absolute pleasure of spending two years coaching "Tulo". Tulo has a big personality, his energy literally fills rooms. He is so much fun to have on your team, in your clubhouse and people just love being around Tulo.

I don't think anyone would describe him as a player that loved or liked to win thou. It would be far more accurate to stay he expected to win. Yes that would be true, but in reality he hated with a fierce passion to lose, he despised, loathed and abhorred losing and that's how he played the game and more importantly it's also how he practiced.

At the time NCAA rules only allowed four players at practice at a time during a period in the fall. As it turned out on Tulo's defensive day his class schedule dictated he had to do his defense practice by himself with the coaches. Occasionally a scout would be out to watch him, but for the most part it was just him.

This is where his unique ability to create his own energy and intensity was on full display. He would literally approach every single ground ball with the same pressure and intensity of game seven of a world series. His mental toughness allowed him to do this for thirty plus minutes straight with no other players around. Tulo fully expected himself to field every ground ball and make every throw with total perfection.

He was constantly competing against himself which prepared him to compete in games. At times he'd make an error or bobble a ball but would instantly go into his routine to quickly learn from that error and almost instantly put it behind him and take on the next opportunity with a clear mind.

How did he clear his mind? For each player this can be different, he might pick up some dirt and hold it in his hand as he thought about that error but when he threw the dirt back on the ground that error was behind him and his mind was back to the next play. Some players take off their hats, some take off their gloves but they recognize and then release that error and use positive self-talk to get focused on the next play.

Ken Ravizza had his system of "the R's", I challenge you to search for those, study them. Many others have different methods. If you want to start owning the moment then start searching and reading. Find a system you like the best and get to work. You can always change but you must start trying.

I've had other coaches tell me they thought Tulo was the most confident player they've ever coached against. I have no way of knowing if that's true. My typical response is Tulo did have one of the best work ethics I've ever seen and was a fearless competitor. His expectations for himself and his team were extremely high. I certainly would agree he was confident but every single part of his confidence was built with his high intensity quality work.

Tulo was simply competing with himself to be the absolute best version of him. In turn his teams became winning teams because to be around Tulo meant to follow him and work or get out of the way. Without yelling or screaming at anyone Tulo just leaned into who he was and created both intensity and energy and most players just followed him because his intent was for the team to be good not just him, it became contagious.

When players ask me how to become confident, I give them a very simple answer: daily put in quality, focused, intense work and win the small things you do every day, it's contagious.

EVAN LONGORIA

Back at Long Beach State we are coming off of the Angels drafting Weaver in the 1st round, the Marlins selecting Jason Vargas in the 2nd round and Evan's buddy and workout partner Troy Tulowitzki in the 1st round by the Rockies.

A little background, Evan was more of a quiet worker, lead by example kind of guy. Extremely reliable and just makes it easy to love his easy way about him. Very calm on the outside but constantly thinking in his own head, very creative, my best description would be he has a unique brain, one of a kind. But, he's also the young man that wasn't even recruited out of high school and went to a junior college for a year. Wait! What was that?

Evan Longoria did not have a scholarship out of high school? Nope. He didn't get to send out a tweet how thankful he was? Nope! None of that happened for Evan. Kids listen up. Evan went to a junior college and worked his tail off. He had a good year and we recruited him. PS: we were not the only school. Then he shows up at Long Beach State and continued to work. He was with Tulo everywhere, working. He listened, improved, kept working and became the 3rd overall pick in the 1st round two years later. Read on.

However, Evan is now entering his second year at Long Beach State; he is coming off an MVP award in the prestigious Cape Cod summer league and is supposed to be the next guy, the next big Long Beach State draft prospect. Imagine the pressure coming from every angle; scouts and agents constantly calling him, evaluating everything he says or does.

This was all new for him, Evan wasn't a guy that had been at all the high school showcases, he didn't play in the acclaimed high school area code games and in fact he had many interests outside the game. He loved his shoes, talked about cars at times and had style to how he dressed. I loved coaching Evan. He was and is a special human. Baseball success hadn't come easy for him and he was open, communicated well and was always ready to improve.

Evan was his own unique person but was constantly compared to Tulo. Shoot, I got tired of hearing it from scouts. Question after question about this player that wasn't recruited out of high school and had gone through two previous drafts completely undrafted. I can't imagine the questions he had to deal with.

There were days I could tell he just wanted to hit and we'd get in the cage and go to work. He would immerse his mind in the drills and the work. We might get through an entire workout and not say a word until I told him great job at the end. He wanted so badly to meet and exceed all those expectations, the physical ability was there. Evan just needed to be Evan and control his mind, his thoughts, routines and self talk.

When a player becomes a high profile draft prospect everything they do starts to matter more. Well pregame batting practice became a bone of contention in Evan's junior season. The scouts would call me and even Coach Weathers would get on me, "what's wrong with Evan's BP (batting practice), it was horrible today".

To this day I still laugh with some of my close scouting friends, I'd hear about it constantly. To be honest there were also days that Evans BP was electric and a complete laser show. However, I still got to the point of actually telling some scouts exactly what we were doing each round. Round 1: 2-hit and runs, 2-runner on 2nd no one out, 1-

runner on 3rd infield in, 1-runner on 3rd infield back and so on.

They would still call, "Mac, Evan's BP?" "I had my cross checker in to see him" and I'd say well did you stick around for the game? "Yes but his BP was terrible", I'd ask, did he get his hit and run on the ground? Yes. Did he execute his situations? Yes. But his free swings he just..... Fill in the blank with whatever they thought.

Now, I've always been of the opinion BP is for the hitter to work on one maybe two specific things, they only get 10-15 free swings on the field in pregame, let's not make this rocket science after all. If needed we can head back into the cage before the game and get more but keep it simple on the field.

As a coaching staff we talked a lot about awareness, being aware of surroundings, situations, how your body and mind felt were important. Evan had terrific body awareness so there were literally days I'd ask him before BP what are you working on and he might say my bat feels slow, I just want to focus on having a fast bat. I'd say ok and move on. I honestly can't remember all the things he may or may not have told me, I had 100% trust in his intentions and goals. He had a firm understanding the scoreboard wasn't turned on yet and BP was for him to prepare for the game.

One day it really bothered Coach Weathers, maybe the scouts had questioned him or maybe it just bugged him more that day. So when I walked into our coach's office before the game we always had versions of the line-up for the game that night. Well not a single line-up had Evan in it. I said, "Coach we can't have Evan sitting on the bench because his BP wasn't good, I might as well go home because we need him". I promised Coach Weathers with everything I had that Evan had a goal and accomplished it in BP. His goal just wasn't the goal everyone else had for him, it was Evan's goal. "Coach, Evan was taking ownership of his career", I pleaded.

Coach Weathers relented and started Evan. As much as I trusted Evan, Coach was showing trust in me, but now the pressure was on. I couldn't say anything to Evan and add even more pressure to him, but I was a little nervous. Evan's first at bat he crushes a missile to left center field and it's over.

From that day on Coach Weathers never asked about Evan's BP again, now the scouts, well they kept coming. However, I will say there was one team that listened more intently when I described what Evan was doing in BP. Remember I always say, it only takes one coach or scout that will fight for you. Well......

Scout Fred Repke, who I didn't know before all this, wanted all the information. Fred knew I loved Evan but he wanted to know why. He never complained about Evan's BP but he would ask me what he was working on, he gathered all the information I could give him. The season progressed. Opponents pitched him like he was already a major league player. Their entire focus was to stop Evan. He'd foul off a good pitch or swing at a bad one, but go straight to his routine and by the time he was back in the box the last pitch didn't matter.

He became totally present in each moment and the only thing existing was the next pitch. Day by day, week by week he made small adjustments learning to control his emotions and thoughts. He grew, matured, started being himself more often and didn't try to do too much. He had a setback here or there but now the entire baseball world was seeing Evan be Evan as his mental toughness increased.

Our season ended but now it was draft day and the Rays drafted Evan Longoria with the third pick of the 1st round and his journey was just beginning and that scout Fred Repke, he was the scout that signed Evan. I know many people have to sign off on a 1st round pick, but Fred had every possible piece of information to fight for his guy. Evan quickly advanced to the big leagues and became a superstar. The kid that wasn't recruited out of high school, drafted as a 20 year old is now 35 and playing his 13th season in the major leagues.

Real world proof, if you never give up, stay positive and keep working, learning, increasing your skills and believe in yourself, then you have a chance. Reminds me of a great book I've read by former Navy Seal Richard Machowicz, "Unleash the Warrior Within" and his trademark statement, Not Dead Can't Quit. Read it yourself, great book.

"CAREER CHANGE"

My coaching stint was coming to a close and I was heading into scouting for the Florida Marlins. I was really excited to get this new journey started. Having a fairly clear idea about the physical attributes needed for prospects. I kept thinking what were the separators? Why did one really talented player succeed when a similar player failed?

I won't bore you with how I arrived with my idea. However, I decided along with the physical tools and what scouts refer to as "make-up". I wanted to identify players that had three specific qualities I thought were separators. I'm not claiming I found some special formula or I identified something new. Many before me likely had better ideas and I'm sure others have used similar ideas, but this was just for me, something I was going to do.

I wanted to find players that loved baseball, all of it: competing in games, developing and perfecting at practice, the ups and the downs. I didn't want some youngster to tell me they loved it. I wanted to see love in action, the kind of love that creates energy and intensity.

Coach Horton told a story about Mark Kotsay when he was playing at Cal State Fullerton. Coach said no matter where Kotsay was on the field at practice, for example down the left field foul line in a bunting station. Coach would start hearing players yelling, cheering and competing because Kotsay had turned up the intensity and everyone was competing to win. Everywhere Kotsay went the energy and intensity followed it didn't matter if it was a game, practice or just guys hitting in the cage.

I wanted that relentless obsession, almost an unhealthy love that keeps guys working when everyone else has left the field. Their actions would prove their love, not any words they used.

Mental game skills developing was something I was going to focus on. Now don't get carried away here, I certainly didn't expect high school kids or even college players to have a fully functioning mental game. However, I did want to see some attempt to stay in the moment, signs of mental toughness and competitive fire. Did they have control of their emotions and how they reacted to a bad umpire call or a teammate making an error?

I wanted to see something they were doing to release tension, maybe try to control their breathing, pick up dirt and toss it back on the ground or take a small break in the action to use self-talk. Minor actions to see they recognized the adversity and were trying to adapt to it and get their minds back under control, mental agility. I wanted signs of mental toughness when things weren't going their way but they never give in, they keep battling.

Professional baseball at the minor league levels is full of every adversity imaginable, bad bus rides, bad hotels, bad apartments filled with players, fields with fans screaming at you for nine straight innings, pitchers giving up three home runs in the 1st inning, hitters striking out four times in a game or an 0 for 25 streak, random injuries, just not feeling right for whatever reason and many other issues.

I wanted players that didn't get angry, pout or throw a temper tantrum every time something went wrong. It doesn't mean I'd eliminate players but maybe I'd put them lower on my list. The more a player was willing to work on their mental skills the more I was able to trust them. It was that simple and I was just trying to separate players with similar physical attributes and believed this would help me.

Ownership of their career was going to be important for me. The most exhausting part of coaching was a player constantly making excuses. It was the umpires fault, my coach's fault, teammates fault, mom's fault, but it was never ever my fault and they are nearly impossible to help.

However, when a player takes ownership of their career they take responsibility for the good, the bad and the ugly. They are accountable for their actions. The way they practice and later prepare before a game is more mature and focused when they own their career.

When a player knows his career is totally up to him, they have great potential to explode and develop fast. They know they have to do it so they listen, learn, pay attention to details and never stop working to improve. Kids will be kids but the ones that really own their career tend to stay away from a bad situation and don't typically find themselves in trouble. I wanted to find players like this.

"SCOUT'S VIEW"

GIANCARLO "MICHAEL" STANTON

At 17 years old he had impressive physical attributes, he could run and throw, but his sheer raw power especially seen in batting practice was jaw dropping. He hit balls in batting practice farther and higher than anyone I'd ever seen at his age.

A tremendous and quite rare these days three sport athlete. He had a strong senior baseball season hitting .393 with 12 home runs and more walks than strikeouts. All of that was great but what we were impressed with the most was between his ears and in his mind.

Mikey as I called him when he was younger had a unique perspective and mental approach to everything he did. First he fully convinced us that he loved baseball and it was his sport. Trust me it didn't take him long to make that clear with the work he put in at practice. We watched as he came off the basketball court and basically right into baseball games and quickly showed the ability to slow the game down in his head and take control of his at bats.

He had a very calm field presence with a fearless yet non-emotional approach to the game. Even when he struggled, he never changed, just kept coming, kept working and most importantly continued to improve. Hit a home run, strikeout or whatever happened he never changed, just kept playing hard. It was fun to watch.

At our private workouts he showed an ability to thrive under pressure, he owned the moment the same way he'd later do at the MLB all-star game Home Run Derby. The only way to have that kind of internal confidence is to put it the work when no one is around, it has to be earned and he earned it.

No matter your size or current abilities there is so much you can learn from him. You've read the stories of him staying in the cages long after games putting in work and will hear about his decision to take notes on all of his at bats. But maybe you are missing the fact that it wasn't easy for him, he truly worked his tail off.

To give you an idea and I wish I could tell you who called me. I can't break his trust, he's a great friend. I love him and to this day a very successful man in professional baseball. But, here is how the phone call went. This 100% a true story and maybe my friend will come out and admit this, who knows.

Mikey was playing in his first pro season in Greensboro, NC. My friend called and said "Mac I thought you knew what you were doing in the scouting profession. I guess you are signing cricket players now. This guy Stanton is terrible, tonight he swung at a pitch that hit the grass out in front of home plate, it didn't even make it to the dirt, Mac it hit the grass".

I remember laughing and telling him not to worry, I was still a believer and Mikey would figure it out. Was I just delusional? Maybe, I'll let you decide. However, the best part was about two months later when my friend called again, this time it was different, "Mac I'm sorry, I was 100% wrong and after these last few months I've seen Stanton do things I've never seen another human do on a baseball field, forgive me I was so wrong". We both just laughed.

The truth is neither of us knew at that time what would really happen with Giancarlo's career. But I can promise you I did know he would never stop working or trying to find a way to be successful. He was fearless and didn't care if he had a setback, he'd just keep believing in himself and keep working.

I don't care if you are 5'6" or 6'5" tall. You can actually work so hard and believe in yourself so much a scout will see you and feel the way I did about Mikey.

It's the same way a man named Al Pedrique felt about Jose Altuve. Here's a quote from Al Pedrique about Jose Altuve, *"But he surpassed all our expectations. More than his hitting and speed, what I most liked about him was his intelligence and heart, and his drive and absolute faith in himself"*. Sound familiar?

I don't know Al, never met him, but I completely understand what he's saying. You young players need to really understand exactly what he is telling you. STOP, player's read this slowly. What I most liked was his intelligence, heart, his drive and absolute faith in himself! Digest that information and really think about it, nothing about his swing, no launch angle or exit velocity. Everything about his mind, heart and mental skills, "HUGE", kids please don't miss this.

CHRISTIAN YELICH

I've never been more proud to have signed a player than I am right now for signing Christian Yelich. Yes, he's going through an offensive struggle. However, he continues to put the work in and play hard for his team. Honestly most of the time his body language doesn't look any different than his MVP season.

Playing baseball can be a roller coaster of emotions. The top players know to perform at their peak level an even kneeled mentality works best. More than just a baseball skill, a life skill is learning to smile in the face of adversity. No one can guarantee future outcomes but I'm not the only one thinking Christian will work out of this.

Every team he faces does. How can I say that? Watch

the way they pitch him, the pitchers are still pitching him like the MVP he is. I will guarantee Christian will do everything possible to work through his funk, I learned this long ago.

Yelly was both the easiest player I've ever scouted and the toughest. Everyone knew Christian could hit and run. How much power? What position would he play? Importantly could he change or improve his long slightly awkward throwing motion? Well he's played all three outfield spots, has hit as many as 44 homeruns in one season and I'll let him dictate the rest of his career. As for his arm action, yes he fixed it by fearlessly and consistently working with some great coaches.

As a scout you can become skeptical and at times you can ponder, "is this young man really this good of a human", sometimes you can start to think this is too good to be true. I spent countless hours asking local coaches, parents, players, students, almost anyone I could find. Everyone basically said the same things.

They say, "Christian is very competitive on the field but he's also extremely polite, thoughtful, and seems to genuinely care about other people." The one thing all the coaches seemed to agree on was they all wanted players like him, but not for his talent they primarily talked about his great attitude.

My boss Stan Meek told me to keep my in-home meeting with him under 15 minutes because he didn't want to alert other teams how much we liked him. Honestly in about five minutes I recognized a personality very similar to Evan Longoria.

Absolutely present in the moment, direct and locked in eye contact. This guy wasn't trying to hide anything or find answers he thought I wanted to hear. Christian was showing I am open, honest and communicating a take me as I am attitude. A very mature eighteen year old and it was beautiful to witness.

Kids today seem to typically have a prearranged answer for almost every question a scout might ask, their answers can be very vague and hold little value. I don't blame the kids, unfortunately they are taught to do it, but Christian didn't have any of that. His answers were straight to the heart of the questions. Christian took complete and total ownership of his career and his answers all reflected that.

Players if you want a scout to fight for you, you need to be as honest as possible. If you don't know something that's better than making up an answer or saying what you think they want to hear. A scout is risking their career when they step up and fight for you. The only way they will do so is if they know you are being open and honest.

Christian and I were once both Marlins, now neither of us are, but I'm still here ready to step up and fight for him! He earned it.

> *These next few players I didn't have the honor or privilege of coaching or signing but they all showed skills at a young age that you the next generation can learn from. My hope is you can use these as examples to follow. We all see players on TV and see how great they are, but the real secret is finding how they got there.*

JP CRAWFORD

It wasn't a secret to those I worked with that JP was and still is one of my favorite players of all-time to scout. I wanted us to draft him badly. It just wasn't meant to be. My story with JP started on a random weekend game at the MLB Academy in Compton, CA. I was down the first base line and even with the first basemen, but this skinny shortstop kept catching my eye.

He'd sprint from the dugout on and off the field, energy bursting through every movement he made. He was showing passion for playing the game, talking on defense, moving around on defense based on the hitters and he seemed to be in the right place all the time. He didn't show any big tools, no cannon for an arm, didn't have super sprinter speed or long home runs at the plate. More than anything his baseball IQ and instincts were drawing me in.

But who is this kid? I had no idea who he was and I had to know. I walked around to his dugout on the third base side and asked the coach if I could talk to one of his players, he said yes this basically just a pick-up game.

As JP came over and I introduced myself I asked him

what school he went to and his answer stunned me. As a scout I knew every school in my area but I'd never heard of this school. JP must have seen the confusion on my face as I asked him, where's that? He answered Lakewood. Now I'm really lost, Lakewood is right next to Long Beach where I was a college coach. About a second later JP looks at me and says, it's a middle school, I'm in eighth grade.

OH my I'm thinking, laughing a little in my head, but knowing this eighth grader is different. He's been out on the field surrounded by high school players but carrying all the energy and passion to win this game that according to the coach doesn't even matter. I'm instantly in love with this player.

JP is still to this day the only eighth grader I've ever given an information card to. Scouts used to use a postcard to get player information like date of birth etc but never before or after did I give one to a player not in high school. A credit to JP, not me. I just mastered the obvious, this young kid loved playing baseball and he was really good.

Funny side note, as I finished talking to JP and walked away my phone rang. It was MLB player agent Lenny Strelitz. He said "you like my guy"? I looked around thinking I was the only person out there scouting that day, but Lenny was there watching JP from a hiding spot down the left field line. There are lessons here for young players and its people will find you if you play the game with the same passion and love JP was displaying for all to see. Most importantly you actually never really know who is watching you play.

As JP entered his senior year of high school, the entire scouting community was on him and knew he was a really good MLB prospect. He had obviously worked to get stronger and all his physical attributes continued to improve. He had separated himself from the rest of players his age and was in a very small group of players being scouted heavily. His physical skills were really good so don't get me wrong, what kept drawing me and many others in was his high energy love of the game, his passion and desire for his team to win. His baseball IQ allowed him to always be in the right place on the field. I continued to rave about him to our scouting staff any chance I had.

One of our cross checkers had flown in to see him a few times and even stated, "all I know is every time I see JP play he makes the best defensive play I've ever seen". I spoke up, "well now you sort of know how I feel, but I've seen him play hundreds of games over five years, imagine the highlight reel plays I've seen".

Back then our staff listened and communicated, it was awesome. We all worked hard and did the very best we could, the draft goes as it goes, it's not someone's fault we didn't get JP. My point is when a player brings his love for the game every day. Plays with pure passion, plays for his team to win not for his own glory, has high baseball IQ and intelligence and he's a good kid off the field a scout will literally fight for that player until his team or another team takes him.

I still love watching JP play and so does everyone around the world, especially those people up in Seattle. Congrats to Demerius Pittman, Philadelphia Phillies scout that signed JP.

BRANDON CRAWFORD

The past is the past, players must decide to learn from it and move on. Brandon Crawford was a really good high school baseball player. He played in the acclaimed area code games and headed to college at UCLA.

He showed himself to be a potential major league player as he was one of the better players in the country his freshman and sophomore seasons. He earned a spot in the prestigious summer Cape Cod Baseball League but struggled that summer batting .189 while making 13 errors in 36 games. Right or wrong, arguments can be made from both sides but in the scouting community performance in the Cape Cod league can hold a lot of weight and determine the draft status of a player.

When he returned for his junior season the love of many scouts for Brandon had gone cold, but I was actually seeing a new player. In my eyes Brandon had a new sense of urgency I hadn't seen from him in the past, a new mature approach with a fire in his belly. I vividly remember a UCLA fall practice at Birmingham high school due to renovations being done at UCLA's Jackie Robinson Stadium.

That night Brandon had different body language, he played with a high energy purpose, he wanted to prove the doubters wrong, and I'll never forget that night. It was a light bulb going on moment remembering players learn, grow and improve. We must allow them time for growth and development.

As his junior season progressed his performance was inconsistent at times. Strikeouts were probably too high, but he was actively making adjustments and working very hard to get straightened out. I saw a shorter improved bat path at times, he just hadn't mastered it yet and the clock ran out on UCLA's season and the draft was here.

One hundred and sixteen players were drafted before

Brandon Crawford's name was called by the San Francisco Giants in the 4th round. For many players of his caliber this could've shaken his confidence but this was a new mature player. Everything he was working on at UCLA started to show in the minor leagues.

All he's done since is help the Giants win two World Series, played more games at shortstop than anyone in Giants history and earned three Gold Glove Awards along with many other awards. Go search for his scouting reports from UCLA available online. The question is did any of those matter? The answer is simple, absolutely not. Brandon took the opportunity he was granted and ran with it, he kept the fire burning inside him and owned his career.

The scouting and baseball community is relying more and more on analytics and metrics. I don't have a problem with that as long as players, scouts and everyone involved remember to value the importance of the size of a player's heart. Brandon proved to all of us his heart is the size of a mountain. I don't really know him and I'm sure he doesn't remember me but I'll be a fan for life. Congrats to Mike Kendall, San Francisco Giants scout that signed Brandon.

"NOT SUPERSCOUT!"

My goal in writing this book is to help players, parents, coaches or anyone that can learn something from it. The last thing I want is for me to be a distraction or come off as claiming I'm right all the time. The last few players I stated facts I happened to really like those particular players. But for clarity I've been wrong many times, anyone in scouting saying they haven't been wrong are either lying or haven't scouted long enough. I have evaluated some players too highly, obviously it's not appropriate to use their names or some like Shane Bieber, Tyler Glasnow, Kevin Pillar and David Fletcher just to name a few I was too low on. Let's dive into those two position players.

KEVIN PILLAR

I've had many people ask me, "If you consider Kevin Pillar to be your biggest blunder as a scout, what was he like as a player"? A really good question. Physically he was a very average high school player and was recruited to a Division 2 school, Cal State Dominguez Hills. He didn't run particularly fast, didn't have an eye-catching strong throwing arm and didn't have great raw home run type power. However, he played good outfield defense which became very good in college, he took very competitive at bats, showed some feel to hit and he played very hard with intent to win baseball games at all times.

Let's quickly remember what I was looking for: talented players that loved the game, had some mental skills and owned their career. I could just kick myself, he had all of those. Sometimes I still question myself, what I was thinking? Kevin had a 54 game hitting streak, was I waiting for 60? I mean I blew it. To hit in 54 straight games takes significant mental toughness, each game the pressure adds and he rolled right through it all. Honestly at the end of every game I saw him play his uniform was dirty from sliding into bases or diving in the outfield.

I really think what I and many in the scouting industry did was underestimate his skills because it was Division 2. Sounds stupid but if I'm being honest that's exactly what I think.

However, if you are a young player here is the good

news, it only takes one scout and for Kevin Pillar that was Kevin Fox from the Toronto Blue Jays. Foxy gets all the credit in the world from me, he did a great job and Pillar rewarded him with a great career on the field.

Kevin Pillar was drafted in the 32nd round, a stunning nine hundred seventy-eight players were selected before him. Did that sink in yet, 978 players were selected before him. Think about that. Yet here I am writing about him. I learned a ton from Pillar and thank him for waking me up and getting me back to my roots. The roots of a player's heart can't be underestimated, ever! If you are a player you should learn as long as you have an opportunity to play, then make the most of it, own it, love it, study it, cherish it and play so hard they literally will have to tear the jersey off you and make you go home.

This book project has nothing to do with me, outside of I'm hopeful this can help some young players reach their goals and get back to having fun and loving the game of baseball. It's the greatest game in the world. If my mistakes help you, then perfect, maybe I won't consider it a mistake but a gift I can now share with others. Sometimes you just have to make a change from your own personal "stinking thinking".

DAVID FLETCHER

David "Fletch" Fletcher was drafted by the Los Angeles Angels in the sixth round. I wasn't really far off on my evaluation, but could I have pressed harder or moved him up some? Probably, like they say, close only counts in horseshoes and hand grenades. So almost getting him isn't actually getting him. However, in scouting you actually get used to not getting all the players you like. It's part of the process and not possible for an area scout to get all the players they like. So why am I bringing up Fletch, because his career is filled with information for you young players. His intelligence for the game is beyond reproach, his love for the game and competitive fire are top of the charts.

Notwithstanding all of David's abilities we have to deal with the reality that major league players are special, many are big, fast and strong. The road to compete at that level is extremely hard and most won't make it. While I'm sure Fletch always wanted to be a big leaguer, he never acted like that was the goal. His goal seemed to be to immerse his entire being into practicing and playing to win.

I was fortunate my nephew was the same age and a local shortstop so I'd see David out at random fields practicing. I'd see him playing for his Connie Mack team. I'd see him on scout teams. Fletch was everywhere, day or night, week days and weekends because he literally loved baseball. I can't remember a single time, not once he didn't look like he was having fun and bouncing all over the field with a positive high energy attitude. If you watched him as a young player that's what you would've seen every single time you saw him.

He practiced and played so much he became an extra coach on every team he played on. His defensive skills were near flawless. He had worked so hard that any ball hit near him was an out. He fielded ground balls clean and released his throw quickly, just ultra polished. That only happens with consistent repetitions and takes massive amounts of time and effort to get that good.

As a hitter he consistently made contact and hit line drives all over the field. He could bunt for hits, take his walks and as a base runner he would take everything the opponent left open. Infielders not paying attention and David would advance bases, pitcher not paying attention and he'd steal a base, he was always looking for an advantage. He became a complete package without any spectacular impact tool.

His high school coach (John Weber, Cypress HS) and college coach (Jason Gill, LMU); both well respected baseball lifers loved him and raved about his work ethic, attitude and ability to lead his team. Much like Kevin Pillar, if you went to see David play there wasn't any one thing that made you say WOW. He just did every small thing above average. He had a simple swing and took competitive at bats, battled to put the ball in play with two strikes, provided productive situational hitting for his team, played fundamental defense and the more you saw him play the more you had to realize there is only one way to be that well rounded and polished. Work your tail off, study the game and love every minute of it.

Many players have reached the big leagues with the exact same story. If you are a young player, be honest with yourself and if you don't have special physical tools, well now you have a person and a guide to follow. David showed you the way, but you must do the work. Congrats to Ben Diggins, Los Angeles Angels of Anaheim scout for signing Fletch.

> *"I never feared about my skills because I put in the work. Work ethic eliminates fear!"*
>
> *Michael Jordan*

"MENTAL SKILLS LIST"

To finish the section off I'm going to list some of the mental game skills I believe you should be working on developing. It takes time but keep working and they will improve. Add more if you want, it would be a sign of owning your career. Did I miss one or two? Maybe I listed too many? It's up to you to decide. In the back of this book I'll add some recommended reading for you to hunt down and find authors you like.

1. Present in the moment.

2. Believe you can do it, that's where action will start.

3. Positive attitude due to your love and respect for the game.

4. Mental agility to deal with change and adversity.

5. Ability to create your own intensity and energy.

6. Mental toughness to never give up or give in.

7. Good work ethic to build your confidence.

8. Ability to use a variety of tools (control breathing/ self talk) to slow the game down, relax, relieve tension and control emotions.

9. Ability to take responsibility and accountability for your thoughts and actions to take ownership of your career.

10. Have fun! Smile. Laugh. Yes there's a time to be serious, but baseball is still a game. Enjoy it.

6TH INNING: SITUATIONAL HITTING

Hello people, is anyone listening? We have a problem. We have to face reality and when situational hitting is only spoken of in hushed tones like seeing a UFO, Bigfoot or the Loch Ness Monster we have a problem.

As I'm currently sitting here working on editing and finishing this project I have the 2021 Dodgers vs. Giants playoff game 5 in the background. Top of the ninth inning score tied 1-1. Justin Turner leading off is hit by a pitch. Gavin Lux now batting, he works to a two strike count and I watch him shorten up his swing and put the ball in play on the ground for a base hit to right field. Runners now on first and second and Cody Bellinger is the batter.

Cody also battled to a two strike at bat. He spreads his feet out a little more, vision is focused, breathing controlled, small rhythmic movements and the pitcher throws a spinning slider in the middle of the plate and

Cody takes a short fast flat swing and hits a rocket through the shift and into right center field. Dodgers take a 2-1 lead on 2 two strike at bats and hold on for the win.

I really hope as you young kids were watching this game that you understand two strike at bats are situational hitting. Tonight proved once again that situational hitting is of extreme importance for your career and team. We saw one team advance and another's season end.

Unfortunately we're starting to only see hitters execute situations during the playoffs. I know we are living in a generation that loves watching long fly balls and home runs but if you value winning baseball games then tonight was a great learning moment. Every team has their own offensive philosophy and I respect that. But teams that can situational hit have always been winning teams.

Let's talk through a few situations and how to be successful. I can promise there are still many college programs that will expect their players to both understand and be able to execute these and hopefully the game at all levels will return to its previous form.

"TWO STRIKE APPROACH"

Do everything humanly possible to make contact with all strikes. Wait! What? Hey now slow down Coach Mac, it's the year two thousand twenty-one and strikeouts don't matter anymore, all the analytic staffs say an out is just an out. Coach you're old school, but we're the generation of three true outcomes, you know home runs, walks and strikeouts. We want maximum bat speed and a good launch angle on every pitch. There is zero and I mean zero reason to argue with this fool's gold idea.

What I will do if you believe this is make you a deal. You can ignore strikeouts and having a two strike approach exactly when a professional organization pays you and tells you its ok. However, if you're banking on that I'll take an educated guess that you won't get enough at bats in high school or college sitting on the bench for anyone to see you play.

To prove to you there is no old school or new school, just the school playing to win. At Long Beach State we didn't always ask our hitters to make a two strike adjustment. We had situations such as two outs and zero runners on base when we'd rather have our guys drive the ball in the gap and get to second base or better. Hitters like Longoria had the physical and mental ability to do that. On a side note, we'd also run in the outfielder's face if we singled in that situation and try to turn it into a double.

However, hitter's that had the ability to steal bases should always do all they can to get on base, so making a two strike adjustment and fighting to put the ball in play makes the most sense. These rabbit's get on base battling with two strikes and then steal second base. It's much easier to score from second base with two outs than it is from first and scoring helps teams win games which is our ultimate goal.

Remember we are trying to come up with the best decision in every situation to win games. Baseball has transformed into a game that has become very productive in having arguments that are NON productive. Every team shows up to win and to win every team should have multiple strategies for multiple situations. Remember what Coach Snow said, "prepare to prepare" for anything, anywhere, anytime.

"WHY BATTLE?"

Let's discuss reasons why we want to fight to make contact with two strikes. You can actually get a hit, yes even a home run. You can put a ball in play creating an error on defense, foul pitches off and drive the pitcher's pitch count up or work to get a walk. Every competitive pitch you force the pitcher to throw creates a higher stress situation and adds a high stress pitch to the pitchers total. The more high stress pitches he throws the faster he will be out of the game. So yes, even an at bat when you foul off a few pitches, maybe get him to throw a ball or two and then finally he just beats you and you strike out is considered a good at bat.

When we were scouting Giancarlo Stanton in high school, it wasn't his long home runs or raw power we were impressed with as his season progressed. It was that he was slowing the game down in the box and when he had two strikes he made contact with pitches that were strikes, at times he would still chase pitches out of the zone but even that was improving. Right before our eyes he was having better team at bats, doing all he could to help his team win.

Scouts can see the obvious big flashy home runs and highlight plays but most are watching the finer details. Those are the details that will matter in three to five years.

"UGH"

"Ugh is a word used to indicate the sound of a grunt to express disgust."

I've heard many say the best two-strike approach is not to allow yourself to get into a two strike count, "Ugh" good luck with that. Doesn't matter what level you play or what percentage of at bats become a two strike at bat. Guaranteed, mark it down every single hitter will get into a two strike at bat situation. What do you do then? Still don't believe me? Here are some facts.

In the 2021 Division 1 baseball season 50.2% of at bats went to two strike situations. The batting average for those was .180, however and now you should be paying attention the BABIP was .317. What is BABIP? BABIP is batting average of balls put in play. So when hitters did put the ball in play with two strikes they hit .317. Still not believing me? How about the 2020 season? 52.2% of at bats were two strike situations. Batting average .167 and the BABIP for those hitters was .309. Thank you to 643charts.com for the statistics. Hitters listen up and put the ball in play with two strikes as often as humanly possible.

"INJURED CORNERED ANIMAL"

Let's work on your mind or mentality to hit with two strikes. I've always used the analogy of an injured cornered animal. How do they act? Ferocious, fearless and quite dangerous!

Typically you'd see this animal spread their feet a bit and get a wider base while keeping much of their mass or weight behind their center of gravity. Their eyes would be laser beamed on their opponent. Breathing controlled and purposeful, no panic whatsoever. They keep their weight back with a little small rocking movement just waiting for anything to enter their attack zone. When it does they strike with short, quick, fast and deadly intent to keep everything out of that zone.

That is your mentality and your two strike approach. Start to imagine pitchers thinking of you as a dangerous two strike hitter. A ball does not get through the strike zone even adding a little bit of room so the umpire doesn't call you out on a close pitch. You are going to fight for the life of your at bat with fierce intent. Most two strike hitting success will be found in your mental skills game.

"LONG OR NERVES?"

If you find yourself reaching for pitches out front with your feet moving all over the place and chasing pitches way out of the zone, one of two things is usually the problem. One your swing path is long and you haven't worked on and perfected a two strike shorter swing path in practice which leads to a lack of trust you have in your own ability.

Easy fix kids, spend more quality time working on this skill. Want to become a team leader, pick a teammate and together commit to meeting everyday either before or after practice for five-ten minutes to work on two strike hitting. Get in your two strike stance and go to battle, help each other, talk about it, shorten your swing. Pitch each other small wiffle balls or use the sunflower seeds we talked about earlier. I promise if you stay committed others will join or start their own. What a terrific example you will be for your team and you will become a better two strike hitter. It's not hard; you just have to do it.

The second problem is when you let fear take over and feel nervous, anxious, frustrated, angry, or panicked because now you have two strikes. Maybe you just fouled off the perfect pitch or you chased a pitch in the dirt and now you have two strikes. Maybe a special person is in the stands and you don't want them to see you strike out.

We'll go through a little thought process example, but remember I had spent a lot of time around Ken Ravizza, along with Jim Skelton, a mental performance coach and also a professor at the time I played at Cal State Fullerton and UC Irvine. Jim is still a good friend, a Ravizza prodigy that has created his own system and is now a Mental Performance Coach for the Texas Rangers baseball organization. You need to do your own research and learning as well.

"BE A LION"

One ball, one strike count and I foul a fastball straight back. In my head right away here's my self-talk, "dang it, how'd I miss that? Idiot you need to hammer that, enough, enough, toughen up, two strikes so what". I take a deep breath in and take my bat, hit my spikes and let the breath go slowly, "lion up". Take another deep breath in and then let it all the way out.

I get my feet in the box and start getting in my stance with my head down "lion", lift my head, arms, hands and eyes up on the pitcher and compete, here we go. Whatever happens next happens. I did everything to get ready and control my career and at bat.

Hey Mac what's this "lion" what's it mean? I always enjoyed animal shows on TV. When I came up with the injured cornered animal I was still a player and what I personally used. I figured a lion, the king of the jungle, was an animal I wouldn't want to deal with in that situation. I still love lions, they're awesome. But it was just my preference, so when I said just the word "lion" in my head it had meaning. I knew exactly what I was telling myself.

When I coached at Orange Coast College I gave our hitters the "injured cornered animal" speech and our pitching coach Dave Bowman loved it and created "tiger up". Our entire team used it, it was terrific, and they all did it. Soon you'll have the tools to create something that fits you or your team.

"REVIEW"

A quick review session, first we have our mental skills we must use. Become fearless. Physically it can vary some player to player. Typically hitters are better served to have a wider base with their feet. You have the option to choke-up on the bat a little if it helps. Keep your body movements small and controlled. Eyes laser focused on pitcher and use your vision skills. Short, quick fast swing at pitches in the strike zone and around the edges some to protect from umpire calling you out.

If the pitch is way outside the zone and the umpire calls you out there is nothing you can do. Let it go, get with your team and get your mind right before going back on defense. Keep it simple. Hitting is hard, hitting with two strikes is immensely hard, but you can battle and be your best by preparing.

"HISTORY CAN BE OUR GUIDE"

I was in high school in 1988 and watched one of the best at bats in major league baseball history live. To say this at bat changed hitting for me is an understatement. This is when I came up with an injured cornered animal and it stuck with me forever.

Kirk Gibson's pure mental toughness was astounding. When you see greatness happen make sure you take it in, digest it and learn from it. Take a few minutes right now to get online. Search for: **Kirk Gibson's 1988 World Series game 1 at bat vs. Dennis Eckersley.** Watch the video. It's a great example of two strike hitting. It also literally shows a player that was injured and just battled. Keep the sound up and listen to the announcers. Enjoy!

I'm hopeful you watched the video and took notes. Did you see any fear? Nope, none! Did he care at all what his swing looked like? Nope. Gibson, who was so injured he couldn't play in this game, but is now facing the best MLB closer of the day. Gets in a 0-2 count quickly, but battles to work the count full at 3-2. Gibson did everything in his power to put the ball in play and came up with a World Series hero moment. Incredible learning moment for all!

"HIT & RUN"

A well executed hit and run play is one of the most exciting in baseball, a huge momentum builder. Typically the hit and run play is used with a runner on first base or runners on both first and second base. The runner or runner's responsibility is to not get picked off and still get the best jump possible. On their 3rd or 4th step they need to peek in at home plate to see if and where the ball has been hit and then adjust accordingly.

The goal of the hit and run play is to move runners up two bases, for example from 1st base to 3rd base by forcing an infielder to cover 2nd base opening up a hole for a ground ball to easily get through to the outfield.

This is a fun time to be a hitter because you know you must swing to protect the runner. The only pitch a hitter doesn't have to swing at is when the ball is obviously going to bounce way out in front of the plate. Anything else, a pitch over their head or way outside hitters must do everything possible to foul it off.

Second rule is the hitter must hit the ball on ground, preferably anywhere not in the middle of the field which would allow an easy double play for an infielder covering second base due to the runner being in motion.

I used to be a stickler for where to hit the ball but with infielders switching who is covering 2nd base and hitters tying themselves up to hit the ball to the right side, I've become more concerned with just hitting it on the ground and out of the middle.

Some very advanced hitters have the ability to see the infielder who is covering and use their bat control skills to guide the ball into the hole that has been created. These hitters are fairly rare, but it is a tremendous skill if you can develop it. The great Tony Gwynn is on record saying he actually would do just this. This is a situational hitting skill that needs to be worked on daily and perfected. You may only get a few opportunities all season, make sure you are prepared to succeed.

"IT'S IMPORTANT"

If you're a player and a coach told you the name of the play is "important". I seriously hope you realize it's imperative you develop the essential skills. Many teams have other names for this situation and I guess I can surmise by watching some teams they don't pay attention to this at all. Likely those that don't use this think we are old school or some other silly name.

The situation is zero outs and a runner at second base. Batters do have options but must execute this play and at a minimum get our runner to 3rd base with either zero or one out. Options are:

1. Swing away but you must hit the ball behind the runner preferably on the ground so the runner can easily advance. A right handed hitter must let the ball get deeper in the strike zone so they can stay inside the ball and drive the ball to the opposite field again preferably on the ground or potentially a deep enough fly ball to right field so the runner can tag up and advance. Lefty batters have it a little easier because they can look to pull the ball. It's an absolute extra bonus if the hitter is able to get a hit allowing the runner to score from second base.

2. Drag or push bunt.

3. Sacrifice bunt but the batter must make the 3rd baseman field the ball so the runner can advance.

The key to all the bunt plays is to angle the bunt straight down so the runner can read the downward flight of the ball and head to third base. This is team offense and the amount of pats on the back and "thata kid" comments in our dugouts were rivaled by hitting a home run. Our teams fed on this and knew the next hitter would do the job to score the runner. Many times our guys would execute with a hit to right field and the outfielder would come up throwing to the plate, miss his cutoff man allowing us to end up with runners on second and third and zero outs leading to our next play.

"HERO"

We now have runners on second and third base with zero outs. Far too often batters try to do too much in this situation. In reality what needs to be done is based on how our opponents set their infielders.

If all infielders play "in" on the grass to stop the runner from scoring then our hitters should look for a pitch and this is true for most hitters should look for a pitch up and middle away they can really drive to the outfielders allowing both of our runners to tag up and advance.

When a defense plays with their corners "in" but middle infielders back a simple ground ball in the middle of the field should advance both runners. When the defense plays all their infielders back it's basically the same, dictating a ground ball in the middle of the field, preferably to the second baseman.

It is important to remember the defense, especially the pitcher, are fully aware we have two runners in scoring position and they are going to pitch you very tough. Hitters should be prepared to see many breaking balls, hard fastballs up and in or maybe change-up after change-up.

You must stay disciplined to get a pitch you can handle for the situation. The absolute worst thing a hitter can do and I don't care how hard you hit it, is to hit the ball at the third baseman. When this happens our runners can't move up and the potential for one of our runners to get caught off the bag increases leading to a worst case scenario. When I see this happen, I can't help but think the particular hitter is very selfish and just proved he doesn't care about his team. Don't be the player giving a college recruiter or pro scout that thought. Instead choose to be a hero!

"RIB-EYE"

You have a big fat juicy rib-eye steak just sitting on the BBQ all you have to do is take it, also known as an RBI. I know I know, we are in a period of time when some consider RBI totals to have less value, but I'm not buying it and neither should you. Anyone that has actually played and knows how hard it is to get RBI's is on my side of this argument. These at bats are much different than hitting with no runners on.

So what exactly is a rib-eye situation? We have a runner on 3rd and less than 2 outs. The infielder's alignment will once again dictate our approach, but as a team we need a high percentage of execution. We've already discussed our options as a batter in the hero section and everything still applies, but now I want you to think outside the box a little bit.

Consider a third baseman either playing back trying to create range or a slow footed one that isn't the most agile defender. We can drag bunt for a hit here and get our RBI and keep the rally going.

Another option, we had a strong defensive catcher that wasn't the most confident hitter but he could really push bunt. He'd get the ball straight to the ground and at the second baseman and score the runner every time. Whether it was important, hero or rib-eye he was likely going to go to his push bunt skill and execute for the team and even ended up with a few bunt hits but always got his job done.

I understand we likely won't see much of it on TV in a MLB game, but every level below these should be options.

Quick note for base runners, if you find yourself on 3rd base with zero outs be on high alert for a pickoff play. Most coaches realize it's very likely you will score so they will take this opportunity to try and pick you off. You must keep your eyes on the ball and know where it is at all times. Don't turn your head away from the catcher. Use your body to take away the catcher's throwing lane to the third baseman. Be alert and do not be surprised by a pickoff attempt.

"RUNNERS IN SCORING POSITION (RISP)"

In the scouting, sabermetrics or really any baseball analysis communities this can be like stepping into a landmine of arguments. The absolute truth is it's an outright skill to be able to stay focused, control your emotions and execute when the pitcher is attacking with an urgent intent. Hitters there are some things you must know to be successful.

First is that pitchers hate giving up runs and will throw the kitchen sink at hitters to keep runners from scoring. They are going to bring their best stuff, focus and effort.

As a hitter you must equal that with focus, relaxation and commitment to your approach. If you have committed to developing your two strikes hitting like we saw and talked about with Cody Bellinger in the playoff game then you have nothing to worry about. Trust yourself and stay committed.

Second, there are times you may need to adjust and look for more off speed pitches earlier in the count, just make educated decisions based on what the pitcher will actually throw. Many of the Southern California colleges will pound hitters with off speed pitches and only throw fastballs off the plate or elevated out of the strike zone with runners in scoring position, practice these situations and be prepared physically and mentally.

Third, always keep in the back of your mind if a base is open they may purposely never give in and throw a good pitch to hit. They will be content to walk you to create a force play if you don't chase pitches outside of the strike zone.

It may be possible you are by far your team's best hitter, maybe the hitter coming up next is playing injured or just not a strong offensive player and you need to be a little more aggressive and open up your hitting zone. This is not a player's decision to make on their own, make sure you talk with your coaches. It's one of the many things I love about baseball, we are constantly provided with a myriad of variables and options. What we decide to do can literally win or lose the game. The biggest at bat of the game can happen in the 3rd inning or anytime throughout the game.

Player's must pay attention to situations, stay locked in to the game and find advantages. It's what the best players and teams do. Finally, once you are in the box you must mentally keep it simple and compete.

7TH INNING: SWING MECHANICS

"TRUST MATTERS"

As we head into the most over discussed part of hitting I want to make a few things clear. First to you critics thinking I'm minimizing mechanics because either I'm too old school or I don't understand the swing so I have to avoid it. You are wrong on both accounts. I've already discussed I'm in the school that loves baseball and would rather work to win games than some silly argument.

I absolutely love helping hitter's fine tune their swing mechanics and have done so many times as a coach and scout. But, I don't claim to have all the answers. Each individual needs to be treated as an individual and most importantly I firmly believe swing mechanics should only be worked on after a player has full trust in their coach's intentions.

Every hitter is different; each has their own strengths and weaknesses. We must let them learn what works best for them and stop forcing hitters to adopt whatever philosophy the coach teaches. Just because Mike Trout does something doesn't mean it will work for every other hitter on the planet. Hank Aaron, Mark McGwire, Sammy Sosa, Lance Berkman, Roberto Clemente, Ken Griffey Jr, Albert Pujols, Edgar Martinez, Chipper Jones, Jeff Bagwell, Nolan Arenado, Freddie Freeman and on and on I could go are first of all very special hitters, but all have differences that worked for them. Don't try to copy their swing, we will try to find what they have in common but just looking like them won't work.

The relationship between a player and whoever is working with them should be one of total trust. I know of many people with fancy titles connected to their name that love to point out what hitters are doing wrong while having no idea how to help them. I'll state this again for you hitters. I don't care who it is trying to change your swing, make sure you check their history. If everything is about their system, only they have the right information and it's not about helping you then run away.

"HAVE FUN"

I've stated this before but it merits being repeated many times, we know factually hitting is hard. Consistently making hard contact with a moving round ball with a round bat is difficult. Getting to and staying in the major leagues is excessively hard and cannot be our goal. Build a solid foundation, have fun, make small changes, have fun, keep developing and learning, have fun and love the game.

Did I say have fun enough? Are you guys listening? If you lose the love and fun in baseball then you're wasting your time. If you are fortunate to stay healthy, have enough talent, mix in some good timing along the way and become a viable prospect I promise you will be surrounded with great options to advance your swing mechanics. Until then, remember to love the entire game, the highs and lows, the streaks and slumps and have fun getting a little better every day. Setting goals and working to achieve those takes time. Be patient, stay positive and keep moving forward.

"STRONG FIST"

I believe everything we do in our swing needs to maximize one of five areas. I like the analogy of five fingers kept together creating a strong fist. When working on swing mechanics our work must maximize at least one of these without hurting the others. They all work together.

1. Vision

2. Rhythm and Timing

3. Balance

4. Strength

5. Bat path and bat speed

VISION

I've talked about vision quite a bit. Hopefully, you understand that I believe even though it's somehow become the least talked about aspect of hitting it's still the single most important. Why? Your vision will help you create your rhythm and timing and plays a large role in bat path (accuracy of barrel contact) and bat speed.

Hand-eye coordination is a primary key to hitting success. Have any of you actually tried to hit with your new swing created by your "guru" with your eyes closed? What's more important to achieve success, a perfect swing or perfect vision? It's something to be considered if you are honestly on a journey to become the best hitter you can be.

Common flaws that can negatively affect vision, late rhythm makes the hitter feel rushed and panic, eyes dance and vision gets blurry. Off balance and vision not as clear as head movement creates different angles eyes must adjust to. Trying to swing too hard or fast creates extra full body effort typically creating head movement forcing eyes to adjust, losing clarity.

RHYTHM AND TIMING

Rhythm is the movements starting your swing. Timing as I stated before can have different meanings for each hitter, make sure to get clarity. For some hitters they talk of being on time in relation to their position to hit (stride foot down with heel spikes in the ground/ hands back). Other hitters talk about contact points, be open to discussion. If it's your swing make sure you know.

Hitters must really learn to understand and increase their body awareness. Learn to discuss when different body parts are moving and where they're moving too. Don't over complicate this, just start to think about your body when hitting off a tee and the more repetitions you do over time, the more you will increase your awareness of your body.

"DANCE"

A very simplistic view of Newton's laws of motion: a body in motion will stay in motion and a body at rest will stay at rest unless acted upon by an outside force is a good example to think about. The extra force if a hitter doesn't have rhythm (motion) will force the hitter to use extra effort to get started, likely having a negative effect on all other areas.

A common flaw for young hitters is to stay in their stance frozen like a statue on top of a trophy until they try to make contact. The problem is hitters don't know what they are keying on to get their swing started. Are they waiting until the pitcher releases the ball? This is likely far too late.

This is why we must learn to dance with each pitcher. A very simple and general way to teach young hitters is to have them follow the pitcher's movements (dance). The pitcher lifts his knee in his delivery then the hitter lifts his knee. The pitcher's throwing hand goes back and then the hitter's hands go back. Pitchers stride foot lands and then the hitters stride foot lands.

Now with their stride foot in the ground, they can start looking for the pitcher's arm and hand in the window frame. This simple drill gets hitters to understand rhythm as they start to get more real hitting experience.

BALANCE

Balance in an athletic position should be an obvious strength. However, many hitters continue to struggle with getting in a strong athletic position which negatively affects vision, timing, strength and both bat path and speed.

We don't need to over think balance but teaching young or inexperienced hitters to focus on being on the balls of their feet and not their heels while keeping their knees bent and head directly above their belly button are a good way to build a foundation. We'll get deeper into this when I talk about getting into a good position to hit, also referred to as a position of power by many hitters.

Common flaws are carrying weight and moving on their heels, rigid straight legs and head getting in front or behind the belly button. But hitters can also lose balance when stride is too long or stride foot is late getting into the ground. A balanced strong athletic position is seen in virtually all sports: linebackers and defensive backs in football, returning tennis serve, basketball players on defense, surfers on their board, downhill skiers and base runners leading off.

STRENGTH

When discussing strength with younger players I try to be very careful and specific. Why? Young players tend to think in regards to big powerlifters, beach muscles and Hercules. Beach muscles are awesome, if you're at the beach.

While Giancarlo Stanton is by far the largest and likely strongest player I've been up close with on a baseball field, I also coached against Dustin Pedroia when he was in college. Pedroia was not physically imposing, some may have called him small, but he was one of the most dangerous hitters in the batter's box and maximized his strength from the ground up. He created leverage.

Hitters I want to identify a few specifics. We are talking about maximizing your own personal strength from the ground up. I try to get hitters to understand they are using the ground as leverage. You want to be focused on the larger muscle groups in your legs and rear end, but a lot of the real work is done by smaller stabilizing muscles especially in your core (midsection) that help with trunk rotation.

Keep your core strong. Every season we hear of players injured and missing time due to an oblique strain. Oblique strains and sprains are very painful and will keep you out of the cages and off the field for an extended period of time. Been there, done that and never want to feel it again.

"PATIENCE YOUNG JEDI"

No, I'm not a Star Wars fan, sorry Mr. Skywalker. Anyway, there's no cheating the process to adding overall body strength, it takes time and genetics are involved. However, you can and should consistently work on adding strength, especially sport specific strength.

Hitters very much need strong hands and forearms but I try with everything I have to keep reminding them core and lower body strength and flexibility must be priority. I had the absolute honor and privilege of watching Ichiro Suzuki focus on stretching and loosening his hip flexors and core for an extra 20 plus minutes before game time when he was still playing major league baseball in his 40's. He's impressive in so many ways but his consistency to keep his body in top form was one of the main drivers to his lengthy career and legacy.

When working with hitters I get them to focus on feeling strong in their balanced position to hit, to feel their feet in the ground and ready to explode. Put your feet in the ground in your position to hit and don't pick them up, now make small movements all around, feel your core, thighs and rear end. Start building a mind muscle connection to whatever their current strength level. This will start to give them a better strong balanced position to maximize vision, balance, bat path and bat speed.

This won't take long to master, but strength in general will. Young kids start small, at our kids camps I would challenge them to start by doing as many push-ups in one attempt as possible, then tell them to do just one more each day and write down their progress. Some days you won't be able to add, maybe even do less. Then out of nowhere you'll do five more then another three and in a few months will have added strength.

Keep at it, challenge yourself, do the same with body weight squats, crunches or planks for time. Pick a few that add full body strength and stability and consistently do them. Learn about getting stronger, ask coaches, read, watch videos and find what works best for you. I promise you will learn and grow, but it's about staying healthy so don't rush or cheat the process.

BAT PATH AND BAT SPEED

Bat path is the route your bat takes from launch through contact and finish. Bat speed simply being how fast it moves through that path or route.

Our bat path is the last thing that happens in our swing so it doesn't have as much of a negative effect on other issues, but they all definitely determine both bat path and bat speed. That's why I'm shocked that so many young hitters are focused solely on the bat path but rarely think about vision, rhythm, timing, balance and strength. My belief is hitters have become far too focused on results without recognizing the importance of the process.

"BARREL ABOVE HANDS"

In any case, there are all kinds of debates and views on what the best bat path actually is. Nonetheless, after coaching, talking with extremely successful major league hitters, scouting a wide variety of hitters and studying and watching countless slow motion hitting videos there are two issues of particular importance.

First it's near impossible to doubt a bat path with the bat knob working down, forward and directly through the baseball with the barrel staying above the hands for as long as possible is what nearly all good hitters do. I only say nearly, just in case an outlier exists somewhere, but that would be extremely rare.

I want to encourage all hitters to watch videos online and find the exact moment the barrel starts to drop below the hands. I promise you will find that most will have their barrel above their hands or a very flat bat, from the knob to the barrel before it crosses their belt buckle. I'm begging you to study this.

Let's get very specific, the barrel will stay above the hands or be flat until the knob is equal to or crosses in front of the hitter's belt buckle. Shall I repeat myself, the barrel will stay above the hands or be flat until the knob is equal to or crosses in front of the hitter's belt buckle. There are variables such as a very low pitch you may find a barrel start to drop earlier, but that will be rare.

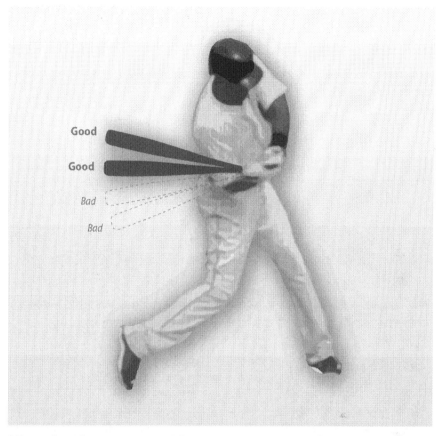

Note that the very next video clip for the hitter above, his barrel will start to drop below his hands, but anytime before that is playing with fire and must be avoided.

Once the barrel drops in it may actually then move uphill due to the plane of the pitch. Take some time and watch MLB hitters slow motion videos from the open side, the vast majority will have a very flat bat from hands to the end of the bat when their knob is at their belt buckle and then will attack the pitch by matching the incoming angle of the pitch.

"GET ON PLANE"

The second issue is getting on plane with the pitch early and staying on plane through contact and finish. We want to match the angle of the incoming pitch and have our bat path on the same plane.

Think about a school room desk, we are going to line up bottles all the way across the desk. The (contact point) is the bottle in the middle but we want our bat path to cut every single bottle on the desk in half. Yes the path might need to be slightly up, no problem.

However, I'm seeing young hitters with a bat path straight uphill that would only be necessary if the pitcher was ten feet tall and throwing the ball directly downhill. It just doesn't happen that way and again we are in need of balance. It may be true that coaches used to teach hitters to swing down on the ball, the old chopping down a tree. Sometimes it was the correct coaching depending on the hitter and the pitcher they were facing. But, we don't need to over exaggerate and create a bat path that is now straight uphill. Have balance, it's where success lies; most bats should be working either fairly flat through the zone or slightly up, "SLIGHTLY".

"REVIEW, THEN STUDY"

I've had people say what about Derek Jeter, he was the master of the inside out swing and I say yes I agree now go watch his video. Even Derek Jeter who had a tremendous ability to let the ball get deep in the zone typically had a flat bat when his knob was even with his belt buckle.

Others have shown me one specific video as proof I'm wrong, but you can't just use one swing on one pitch. I've seen Miguel Cabrera hit a ball very down in the zone and his barrel was low early but again the pitch was down just below his knees.

Many players and people aren't willing to try and find the truth and just like to argue. I have zero interest in that. I'm honestly just trying to help kids, not push some point of view. I don't mind being questioned or challenged, in fact I love it. However, you must do the actual work of studying and working with hitters before having strong opinions based on virtually nothing but random theories and opinions.

"TRUTH"

There are many great quotes on truth and honestly I don't know who gets credited with this one but its good. "The truth doesn't mind being questioned. A lie doesn't like being challenged." Let's agree to find what is true and be open to continue learning as we age and grow. It's literally the key to developing and improving in life.

So what actually happens when a player loses their barrel too early? They open multiple holes in their swing on pitches they physically cannot hit. They slice softly hit balls to the opposite field they should drive to the middle of the field. They tend to pull balls with top spin, many on the ground because they will have a need to roll their wrist early and at contact their palm on the top hand is facing down when it is preferable to have the top hand palm facing up and bottom hand palm facing down to the ground at contact.

The simplest and best bat path is one that the barrel stays above the hands for as long as possible and stays on the plane of the ball the longest. Hopefully we can all agree and move forward as we continue to learn together.

"FAST, STRONG BAT"

As for bat speed, it can and will improve as vision, rhythm, timing, balance and strength improve. Most kids try to add strength with effort but without the others you're just fighting against yourself. Everything works together and hitters must learn to stay connected, a term I will discuss more soon.

There are drills to improve a player's bat speed. I've used many with kids. I've tried things that just didn't work. For me the best single drill is one I picked up from Manny Ramirez. Yes, the Manny Ramirez that played 19 years in MLB, 12 time all-star, 555 career home runs and .312 career batting average, look him up, watch his videos.

A good friend was a minor league player and prospect with the Indians. He took me to Angel Stadium when the Indians were in town. As it happened we were there very early, it was the mid 1990's and stadium security was more open. My friend had a meeting to talk with Charlie Manuel, the Indians hitting coach.

As we walked up and Charlie talked to my friend, Manny was there hitting off a tee. Charlie called Manny over and said, "Hey Manny this kid is going to come take your job". Manny smiled and said "I hope so" and went back to hitting.

We watched as he hit balls off the tee with a huge weighted doughnut on his bat. One of us asked why the huge doughnut? Manny responded essentially through his strong accent, "helps me control my barrel and makes my bat fast and strong". Good enough for me, one of the best hitters alive gives advice, I'm taking it and later as I head into coaching or working with hitters I'm sharing it.

Now we should know we are trying to maximize our vision, rhythm and timing, balance, strength and bat speed and bat path. It's time to move into the actual swing sequence.

SWING SEQUENCE

Hitters please listen and take heed. Do not get so consumed with the mechanics of your swing that you quickly find yourself in the spiral to failure. I've seen more hitters get stuck in their own heads worried about mechanics than any other aspect of becoming a fearless hitter. Keep it simple, take it one day at a time and be patient with the development of your swing sequence.

"STAND ON YOUR HEAD"

The old saying "if you can stand on your head and hit, I'll let you" is one I'm in agreement with. The only reason to worry about stance is if it creates an obvious complication. My two simple rules have always been 1. Get both eyes on the pitcher 2. Stance should allow you to easily get into a good strong position to hit.

"STACKED"

I would typically like young players to learn to hit from a stacked stance. Feet shoulder width, knees inside feet, hips above knees, shoulders above hips with their head directly above center of gravity.

For older more experienced hitter's I leave it up to them unless a red flag pops up. Everything else is style. Many players will adjust their stance on their own as they develop as the pitching gets tougher.

I would warn players not to visit the stance store over and over again. Meaning don't make a change just for the sake of change, this will create inconsistency that is hard to overcome. Furthermore, you will never know what is working and what isn't. When you make a change stick with it for a period of time and evaluate after giving it a chance.

If you have committed to the two rules then it's highly unlikely your stance is the problem. MLB players for years have shown us very unique stances but they always have a reason. Do NOT create a stance just so you look unique.

"GO BACK BEFORE GOING FORWARD"

Some coaches may call this getting gathered or storing weight. These are typically smaller movements made completely under control, everyone is slightly different but in general here is what should happen.

As a hitter's front foot is coming off the ground, they should be transferring weight back into the inside part of their back leg with a slight inward front hip turn. This movement should be controlled, slow and easy. As a rule I like to say to hitters you must go back before going forward just to instill a verbal cue.

If you see or if a hitter can feel their back knee either straighten out or bend back towards the catcher that would be considered transferring weight over their backside and needs to be corrected quickly. Hitters need to learn to really feel they are storing weight on the inside of their back leg in order to control their stride.

Things to look for on the positive side would be a slight bend in the back knee and a majority of hitters will have their knee slightly inside their back foot.

I will say Evan Longoria was one of the few hitters I've had that had his knee directly over his back foot at times, but he kept a slight bend and his knee never went back towards the catcher. Getting gathered was very important for Evan and it should be for all of you. This move back allows you to control your stride while also being able to maximize your vision enabling you to land your stride foot on time.

"GETTING INTO A GOOD POSITION TO HIT/ POSITION OF POWER/ STRIDE SEPARATION"

As your stride foot reaches forward your hands move back in the opposite direction. Why did I say reach? In order to keep hitters from pushing all their weight forward I use reach. Hitters can think about their hip flexor stretching out as the foot moves forward.

As the hands are moving back, it's desired to keep a slight bend in both arms at the elbow. However there are rare hitters that have been successful when their front arm straightens out, known as an arm bar. Arm bars are difficult to succeed with so if possible work to keep a slight elbow bend.

As your stride foot begins to softly land on the ball of your foot, you should start to feel a stretch from your front hip flexor through your core to your rear oblique. By keeping your focus here it will help to reduce the potential issue of an arm bar.

Many teach hitters to visualize they are stretching a rubber band from their stride foot to their hands. This can lead to a hitter pushing their hands straight back creating an arm bar so I stay away from using it.

Many young hitters will land on their tippy toes and don't get their heel spikes in the ground on time. I see many young hitters weekly and a high percentage are late getting into a good position to hit. Understand if you are too early you can still survive. However, if you are late it's game over.

"POSITION OF POWER CHECKPOINTS"

Now as we have our entire stride foot in the ground and our hands back we feel the stretch through our middle, again front hip flexor through the core to the rear oblique.

It's important to understand: your heel spikes on your stride foot must enter the ground while being stretched in the middle with your hands back before you are considered separated and in a good position to hit.

In a good position to hit you should be in a strong athletic position with familiar checkpoints. Feet outside knees, hips above knees, shoulders above hips, head above belly button in your center of gravity, knob of bat pointing downward in the direction of the catcher and the end of the bat close to being directly over the middle of your head. We have now built a very strong foundation for our swing.

"SWING"

You are separated and in a position of power, it is this separation that will allow your entire body to stay connected and strong through this sequence.

The swing works from the ground up. As your front heel spikes enter the ground, your back heel will start to come off the ground. Remember that word "leverage", we are keeping our weight behind a strong front leg and transferring our strength from the ground into impacting the baseball.

The swing sequence starts from your back knee, then

hips and your hands follow last. Many use terms like turn your back knee, I'm always hesitant with this because many young hitters will then just spin their entire body. While that does work for some hitters, we must remember hitters are different and as a coach I've found other terms to be more useful until the hitter really understands what works best for their swing. So I'll tell young hitters we want our back knee to point at the ball and then our back hip points at the ball and then our hands can stay inside the ball as our barrel cuts the ball in half.

We can have a long discussion on rotational versus linear hitting, but the truth is both ways work for different hitters and some great hitters combine both. Again, I'm here to help all hitters, not just the ones that believe in my philosophy. Facts are facts and both rotational and linear hitters are in the Hall of Fame.

As discussed earlier the bat knob will work down, forward and directly through the baseball with the barrel staying above the hands for as long as possible.

During this entire sequence our head should stay over our center of gravity (belly button) which is staying behind the ball.

As for your finish or follow through, just make sure you let your hands and bat continue through contact without yanking them hard off the ball. We've seen many great hitters finish their swing up high over their shoulder, but George Brett rode his lower finish to the Hall of Fame in Cooperstown. So do what comes natural with your finish and adjust as needed.

"SIMPLIFY"

Kids when coaches repeat themselves they are trying to get you to really pay attention. So once again, keep it simple. I've always tried to keep this process as simple as possible and many times have repeated the following sentence. "Trust your plan, use your eyes, and get into a good position to hit, stay behind the ball and have a loose, easy, fast swing."

I completely understand I'm veering off current day slogans of create launch angle, load your scap, swing as hard and fast as you can from an over manufactured position to hit and I'm fine with my decision.

Studying hitting and the game of baseball I've learned success goes to those that find balance. The balance between maximizing bat speed while also maximizing consistent barrel contact is one of many truths I've found in the magical game of baseball to be important for successful hitting.

One final thought on swing mechanics for you young hitters to consider before attending your next practice or game. Agree or disagree, it's your choice. A hitter can have great mental skills and bad swing and still hit. They cannot have a great swing and bad mental skills and hit. You should know by now what my choice is. Focus only on your swing to your own peril. Food for thought, something you youngsters hanging around these hitting gurus should consider.

8TH INNING: THE WHOLE STORY

"HUMANS NOW RIVAL GOLDFISH"

We're living in an era where quick and short video clips inform us of many topics. We read headlines and think we know what happened. Society now has an attention span as long as a goldfish, actual studies state we as a society are down to an 8 second attention span. I appreciate the efficiency of short videos as much as anyone, but we're not getting the full story to literally anything. We watch 10 seconds and think we understand something. That's crazy!

It's impossible to understand hitting that quickly. Certainly impossible to comprehend what it means when we hear a hitter has revamped his swing, but now is dominating. First we only hear about the success stories, not the many players that had career ending swing changes. Those names are forgotten forever and their guru's never speak of them again.

However, what we are going to do is pick a handful of the most well known MLB players swing changes and try to find out the whole story. We are going to research and find what they have in common and search for what we can learn from them and potentially add to our hitting arsenal.

JUSTIN "RED" TURNER

I had the pleasure of watching Justin as a high school player and the torture of coaching against him in college. He was one of the most competitive, high baseball IQ amateur players in the state. He started at Cal State Fullerton his freshman season and every year after. It was a rare feat to walk into a then powerhouse program and not only start and play every day but also excel from day one.

It was obvious in the dugout versus him he had good vision and wasn't fooled easily, his freshman year even walking more than he struck out. He had good takes on pitches out of the zone and was typically in a balanced position to hit on time. The thing he did really well was make consistent contact on his barrel. He showed a tremendous feel to hit and what looked to be plus hand eye coordination. Although I would have no idea what his plan was or his approach we knew he stayed committed to his plan because he was so hard to get out.

You can take a look at his and other player's stats on baseballcube.com or other sites and see Justin routinely had batting averages over .300 and even early in his pro career many (OPS) in the .800's.

Many are probably asking what (OPS) stands for. On base percentage plus slugging is a newer way used to measure the value of a hitter's at bats using addition. On base percentage + slugging percentage= OPS, it was designed to identify or judge a hitter's ability to both get on base and hit with authority.

Many of the "new" school kids like to use OPS, I'm personally still a fan of batting average, on base percentage, RBI's, doubles and home runs but let's go ahead and speak their language and hope a light bulb goes off in their head. A perfect opportunity for all of us to get together, learn and improve.

Justin's OPS started to drop early in his major league career and then according to his own interviews stated in 2013 he started changing his approach and prior to 2014 revamped his swing. It's been fun to watch one of Southern California's favorites go from an average part time player to a star. I'm sure most of us that coached against him couldn't be any happier for him. I do have questions though.

I wonder if he didn't have such good vision, hand eye coordination and ability to make barrel contact if all the changes would've worked. I wonder if he didn't understand how to dance and battle versus the pitcher, some may call it understanding the art or feel for hitting if it would've worked. I don't know if he thought about hunting pitches and looking for contact points in college but it sure looked like he did and now he's just made adjustments to hit the ball more out front. Also of note, he has stated he actively tried to hit the ball in the air more often. He said with his lack of speed he wasn't going to get any infield hits and needed to drive the ball more often.

Many of these questions we can't answer, but we can look at others that have made successful swing changes and take a look at their before and after and search for what we may find.

JD MARTINEZ

We're all in the same boat here as I have zero history with JD. I never saw him play as a younger player, so this time let's use baseball-refrence.com. We see he signed as a 20th round selection so the expectations for him weren't all that great. But, oh my, he destroyed minor league professional baseball his first two and a half seasons. Regularly having batting averages around .340 and OPS well above .900 and entered the big leagues as a 23 year old in his third season of professional baseball, very impressive.

The next two seasons were not as kind to him, but he says he started figuring some things out in winter ball at the end of 2013. However, he was still released by the Astros in spring training in 2014. What may seem like a mistake for the Astros was the best thing that could happen for JD and potentially he never would've become a star in Houston. JD landed with the Tigers starting in triple A and then arrived in the major leagues and never really looked back.

He has stated, "he has a swing he taught himself", I love that he became his own hitting coach with the help of others but he owned it. JD claims to constantly watch video and evaluate his own swing and stays committed to getting on plane with the ball as soon as possible. Since he says he wasn't blessed with a great swing he has to critique himself and grind it out working hard.

He credits watching Miguel Cabrera hit as helping him learn about a good swing and learned to prepare from Victor Martinez and Torie Hunter so we are learning he took advantage of learning from the elite players around him.

So what else have we learned? JD had a pretty high level of success early on in his pro career and showed a solid ability to hit, but needed to become a better version of him. He already had a good understanding of how to approach the battle versus pitchers but needed to overhaul his own individual swing mechanics to make it work for him. According to him he did make a concerted effort to drive the ball in the air more often and worked extremely hard to be consistent with his swing. This is another great story we can learn many things from but let's study a few more before we make any conclusions.

JOSH DONALDSON

Josh was also a very talented amateur player. He went to Auburn University out of high school and not only played but had a good freshman season in the SEC. His performance continued to improve and he was drafted in the 1st round by the Cubs. Josh was putting up solid but not superstar numbers in the minors and arrived in the big leagues in 2010, for the next three seasons he would bounce back and forth between triple A and the majors. However, at some point in 2012 he started making swing and approach changes and from 2013 until present day he has become a MLB superstar.

Josh has been very vocal about his swing and why he does exactly what he does. Unfortunately many kids have tried to copy his difficult movements with very little success. When searching through his career stats you see a player that never had a problem with striking out and regularly had good walk totals. These simple facts lead me to believe he has good hitting vision, an awareness of how pitchers will attack and a good approach to hitting.

Kids, you can't just copy his movements without having the other skills he already had, not to mention his skills were very advanced.

When watching his actual movements what do we see? He has big movements, a high leg lift and fairly long downward hand pump. Then as he gets separated his hands work back and up while he does have a longer stride than most, he lands in a really good, strong and balanced position to hit.

Josh does a tremendous job of creating strength from the ground up and a fairly traditional sequence with an extremely fast bat that works on the plane of the ball. He has good extension through the ball and many would say he does a great job of cutting the ball in half. Although he does hit many balls in the air his path is only slightly uphill and more accurate to say he stays on the same plane as the pitch without trying to overtly lift the ball.

Some of the things Josh has said in interviews are extremely important for young players. Unfortunately I think players have watched his highlight videos without actually listening to what he has to say.

I'm going to highlight a few: Josh has stated it's extremely important for hitters to have body awareness and know exactly what their body is doing during their swing.

He spoke about hitters needing to know what rhythm and timing mean to them. He consistently states hitters should be asking why they are doing whatever it is they are doing.

Finally, Josh stressed the importance of hitters really understanding exactly what their best swing is. Great information for kids, thank you Josh for trying to help!

JOSE ALTUVE

Let's just state the obvious, Altuve is a great hitter and has always had way above average hand eye coordination. Jose was a successful hitter in the minor leagues and arrived in the big leagues at the young age of 21. He has consistently improved each year.

I'll quickly deal with what many are thinking. Did he and the Astros cheat? Who knows what the actual truth is? The way I see it is it's not why we are here, we will never know the truth and at this point it's just a distraction for us. Frankly, I don't let myself get sucked into things that have zero bearing on what I'm doing and we need to trust those in charge will get to the bottom of it. We can't do anything about any of it, so let's not waste any more time worrying about it.

As a young player he was a very aggressive swinger, didn't walk much and didn't strikeout, just collected hits all over the field. So what did he do to get his power?

The first and most obvious thing that happened is he got older. At 25 years old he started to increase his home run totals and has continued as he has increased what we call, his man strength. He's matured and obviously worked on full body strength. Youngsters stay patient because you will get stronger as you age and work at it. Keep your focus on learning to hit while also committing to getting stronger day by day.

As for swing changes and researching him you will find he worked hard to keep his body in motion. Early in his career he would stride early and his body would stop which required him to start again.

Remember Newton's law, a body in motion stays in motion. The addition of his slight leg lift has helped him achieve his goal of staying in motion. Doesn't mean a leg lift will work for everyone but it has helped Jose. I'm positive he has made many small adjustments through the years like all major leaguers but none have had the impact of his new approach.

Listening to Jose, he says he worked hard to become a more selective hitter. He decided to hunt for and attack pitches he could drive and stopped swinging at everything in the strike zone. Jose was able to increase his ability to take pitches that were strikes but ones he couldn't drive and is actually increasing his power by swinging less often. No doubt this controlled aggressive attack plan has also helped his power numbers increase. Jose is also on record saying he studies the pitchers he will be facing which has helped him create his attack plan.

So what are we finding? Yes he has made some positive swing changes, but the driving forces for his power surge point to his body maturing while adding strength, his more selective attack plan to get pitches he could drive and his ability to actually not swing at strikes if he wasn't looking for that pitch. There are so many valuable lessons in his story we can focus on and learn from.

AARON JUDGE

A very familiar pattern emerges when looking at Aaron Judge's amateur career. He was drafted out of high school but decided to head to college. As a freshman at Fresno State he hit .358 and played nearly every game. He followed up with a summer in the Alaska league hitting .298 and as a sophomore at Fresno State hit .308 while walking more than striking out.

Did he have big home run numbers? No he didn't. However, I can tell you he did have one of college baseball's best hitting coaches in his head coach Mike Batesole and was just getting started. Aaron headed to the Cape Cod Summer League where he hit .270 with five home runs in 100 at bats and was about to explode.

In his junior season he hit .368 with an incredible 1.117 OPS, including 15 doubles, 4 triples and 12 home runs. The Yankees selected him 32nd overall in the 1st round.

Once again we are seeing a very talented young player, in addition to one receiving foundational instruction from a very experienced and skilled coach. Aaron has continued to have solid or better batting averages, has always had good walk rates and although his strikeouts have received negative comments it looks like he may be on the verge of improving. But, where did all the home runs come from?

I always like to master the obvious and the reality is Judge is a huge human with tremendous strength. At 6'7 tall and weighing in over 270 pounds we can safely assume the home run strength was just waiting to be tapped into.

Early in his career he stayed tall in his stance, didn't get into a great position to hit and his bat path was in and out of the zone rather quickly. All of that including his sometimes poor pitch selection and he was still athletic enough to have a ton of success.

In 2016 he added a new leg kick and was getting his bat on plane earlier and longer. Aaron has continued to make small adjustments to his swing and credits getting into his legs better which has stabilized his head helping him continue to improve his bat path and pitch selection. In

2021 he added a new and improved 2 strike adjustment which showed success and we all hope he can continue.

I am purposely staying away from the drama online and social media revolving around who gets credit for the changes to his swing. First, from all accounts Aaron Judge is a superstar human being and he deserves to be treated that way.

Second, I think I've made it clear I believe it takes a village to help these young players develop and succeed. I'm sure he had many people along the way help him and I know his college coach is a great one. I just wish we'd give the credit to Aaron, his family, friends and for the rest just be happy if you played a part in it. Remember it's supposed to always be about the player and he's one heck of a great player we can all support.

"WHAT HAVE WE LEARNED?"

While it's very true all of the above hitters made changes and a big part of those changes was to drive the ball in the air. However, when you listen to them talk they use descriptions of driving the ball off or just over the center field wall, not high towering routine fly balls. This huge difference keeps them driving through the ball on the plane of the pitch, not swinging underneath and lifting the ball.

What else did we learn and I hope you young players take this to heart. We learned many, in my opinion, most successful swing overhauls only happen after a hitter has a strong and complete foundation as a hitter, not a swinger, but a hitter. Their vision, understanding of contact points and approach were very advanced while also already having many mental skills to help them through these new adjustments. That foundation as a hitter was built through hundreds, sometimes thousands of at bats as youth, high school, college and even professional players.

They had already proven to themselves they knew how to battle versus a pitcher giving them the much needed true confidence to complete this new swing change. This is of utmost importance and young players must really face this reality before jumping into a cage with some guru to make full scale changes to their swing.

These hitters also were either fully matured or very close and had the "man strength" that comes with it. Let's face it, the most famous hitters and their swing changes happened when those players were in their mid-twenties, not at 8 to 15 years old.

I'm not saying hitters shouldn't make changes until they are also in their twenties, but rather make one change and master it before making another. Having a new and improved swing takes time, a lot of time and focused effort.

Younger players don't have the time or mental capacity to completely redo their swing. These professional players spend hours a day, day after day, week after week focused solely on their swing overhaul. Younger players are still in school, need to have friends and some social life, they need to be kids. They don't have the hours, days or the mental skills to make these changes.

I've seen many try, it's painful to watch and a majority end up finding the spiral to failure. "Patience young Jedi" isn't just some slogan I use with hitters to try and be funny, I mean it, young hitters must be patient with their development of becoming a fearless hitter with a good swing.

"BONDS, BARRY, BONDS!"

My brain works differently. I actively question just about everything and try to find certainty while lining up as many facts as possible.

Constant questions fill my head as I hear others speak. Asking: Why? Is it really true? Is it that simple? Does it need to be this complex? Are there unintended consequences? Is there a better way to do it? Is something more effective or easier to complete? Is there a path of least resistance we aren't seeing? Is this person just making this up? Are there actual facts behind what they are saying?

Let me ask you a few questions. Did we find one perfect swing everyone should do? My answer is absolutely not! Why do all these hitting "gurus" have to use videos of the best hitters on planet earth? Have they or you considered those best hitters in the world have special hand-eye coordination? Is it possible these hitters have elite and uncoachable vision to brain to body connections? Is it possible the only way to develop this vision to brain to body connection is through hundreds, maybe thousands of real at bats and not cage swings? Does everyone realize these hitters have some of the best bat speed in the world? Could superstars have elite rhythm, timing and balance? Is it possible they have an internal baseball clock unlike the rest of us? Food for thought, I know my answers, now it's up to you.

Should gymnastics coaches teach all gymnasts to be like Simone Biles, Nadia Comaneci or my personal favorite Mary Lou Retton? Does every quarterback have to throw like Tom Brady? Kareem Abdul-Jabbar is the NBA all-time scoring leader but no one else uses his sky hook shot. Why?

Was that shot something only he could consistently do?

Go watch videos of Hall of Famer Joe Morgan hitting. Why hasn't anyone copied his back elbow movement? 5'7 and 160 pounds, played over 20 years in big leagues, won a couple MVP awards, not worth a try? Probably not, it worked for Joe and likely only Joe. Consider all of these as you think about hitting and work on being the best version of you.

All these gurus seem to use videos of Barry Bonds, Albert Pujols, Mike Trout, or whoever is the flavor of the year. Mark my words videos of Vlad Jr. or someone else dominating will be everywhere very soon, the gurus need to ride the wave of fame to get people to watch their videos and listen to their "special" breakdown.

Yet with all of this information we have to ask. Do Judge, Altuve, Donaldson, Turner look entirely different and do entirely different things? Yep. So what's the answer we are looking for?

These hitters did exactly what they needed to do to improve. The changes they made were tailored specifically to them. Aaron Judge didn't copy Mike Trout, JD Martinez didn't copy Roberto Clemente, Vlad Jr. didn't copy Bonds, Barry, Bonds.

Each player does what is going to work best for them and them alone. I can watch Bonds videos for hours. I love watching him hit. Others probably say the same thing about Paul Goldschmidt, Mark McGwire, Sammy Sosa or Will Clark. But I'm not naïve enough to think I can do the same thing or teach others to hit like them.

Young hitters this is very important. You must focus on becoming the best version of you. Think about some of the unique hitters we have seen in the major leagues and pull up videos of Jeff Bagwell, Rod Carew, Wade Boggs, Tony Gwynn, Rickey Henderson, Gary Sheffield or Frank Thomas. I mentioned Joe Morgan earlier; take a look at his walks versus strikeout stats, obviously all special players. However, they all went about their work their own way.

Yes they have similar traits, many or all we have covered but don't copy their every movement, that's crazy! Certainly don't let someone have you do everything a major leaguer does, you aren't them.

If you don't have years of experience, how will you know what to change? The answer is you won't and will have to rely on the person coaching you. It should be very clear to you why I believe trust is a huge factor. If you are considering a swing redo you better trust this person with your entire career because if by chance they pick the wrong changes for you, then unfortunately your baseball career could be over and they will forget about you as their next victim walks through the door.

9TH INNING: BECOME YOUR OWN HITTING COACH

What can you do? How do you become your own hitting coach? Last player story; the first call I received from player development was from John Mallee. Mallee was the Marlins minor league hitting coordinator and is now a major league hitting coach for the Angels.

Remember this was my first year of scouting and Mallee is calling me. I remember him saying, "Hey Mac I wanted to talk to you about Stanton". It was about this time I felt my heart beating through my chest, Ooooo no I thought. Stinking thinking on my part, the reality is Mallee called to tell me Stanton was taking ownership of his career and actually taking notes in his own personal notebook on every single at bat he had in the minor leagues. Mallee was blown away and pumped to see the big guy getting after it. "Mac go find us more just like this kid", I could hear the enthusiasm in his voice, what a great feeling. Thank you "Male's"!

WHAT'S A GOOD AT BAT?"

Understand Stanton was taking complete ownership of every single at bat, a great example of becoming your own hitting coach. The question becomes how do you accurately evaluate yourself?

Unfortunately, many of you are stuck on results. If you get 3 hits you bounce around smiling after the game, even if your team lost. If you don't get any hits, you walk around like you found out the world is ending even if your team won. The pressure is overwhelming, you can't win. Sad, defeated and depressed because of the decision you made to rely on your personal statistics. You just found another spiral to failure putting yourself in that dark and lonely mental hole.

There's a better way and parents you play a significant role. Your questions better be good ones or just blame yourself when they quit playing the game they once loved. It's a long journey, stay positive. Simple questions to ask: Did you have fun and give your best effort? Did you improve today? How? What did you learn in today's game?

Players we've already discussed many areas in this book to evaluate: Are you seeing the ball better? Can you recognize pitches earlier? Are you developing better control of your breathing? Did you feel confident? On and on you should be able to go.

Let's talk about a few specifics for each at bat, as always feel free to add your own. Keep it simple, goals you can control and achieve. Did you have a plan, were you prepared for the situation and did you execute? Did you give your best effort to help your team win? Did you hit the ball hard? Did you make the pitcher work? Did you fight to stay positive, even when things weren't going your way?

No excuses, be honest. You weren't unlucky, unless you were playing the lottery. Competing is hard, sometimes you do everything right and still fail statistically. Are bloopers and swinging bunts really better than hard hit outs or a hard fought two strike at bat in your development? You might feel better today, but are you becoming a fearless hitter? No, it's short term happiness that will set you up for long term pain. Look up Steve Springer; he's been talking about this topic for years: Qualityatbats.com.

Don't get me wrong, we all take the hits when they come, but they can't determine our attitude. Continue to monitor if you're making progress in becoming the best version of you. It's a long journey and why you must get mentally tough to stay positive, keep the fire burning and get back to work to improve for the next at bat or game.

It's time to send you off. You can become the best version of you. Be present in the moment. Today, take an active role in your own development. The best hitting coach you will ever have is YOU!!

"STEPS"

1. Have fun: remember you are supposed to love this.

2. Positive mindset, believing you can do it will start your actions.

3. Own your life and baseball career and never give up.

4. Win in your daily activities.

5. Practice your vision skills.

6. Master your contact points.

7. Develop your approach, own the middle 12-14 inches of the plate.

8. Master 2 strike hitting.

9. Add mental skills to your mental toolbox daily.

10. Study pitchers of all levels.

11. Learn the game. Talk with coaches about situations.

12. Work on your skills: bunting, hit and run, etc

13. Learn to hit the ball on the ground or in the air whenever you want off a tee, in soft toss then batting practice to be ready for the game.

14. Work on your rhythm; learn what body parts are moving when, where and why.

15. Know what being on time means to you.

16. Develop balance and strength throughout your swing.

17. Work on the best bat path for you.

18. Develop faster hands and bat speed.

19. Accurately evaluate your at bats, not just the results?

20. Ask why? Start with these 20 and you are well on your way to being your own hitting coach.

21. There are 21 outs in many youth and high school games, so I'll take this one moment and remind all of you to work just as hard at developing your defense.

Please!!! I'm begging you; don't make your plan to hit your way to the big leagues. Be well rounded as a baseball player.

POSTGAME TALK

"A QUICK FINAL NOTE FROM ME TO YOU."

Hitters, I certainly don't know everything about hitting and I'm positive I missed things in this book. I am neither the world's leading hit doctor nor a great writer. I just want to help as many of you as possible. I love hitting and everything that goes into it.

I'm still learning everyday from many different sources. Be open and coachable. There are many great coaches with great advice. Most love their players. Learn to listen, but don't be afraid to ask questions. I had so many great coaches who changed my life a thousand positive ways. It's ok to try new things, just be thoughtful. Think things through. Ask questions.

Finally but maybe most important: Love this journey you are on. There isn't a final destination where now you are a perfect hitter. Be patient, stay positive, keep working and learning. I truly hope this helps you become a fearless hitter and gives you ideas to develop your skills in a variety of ways. Love it and have fun. Coach Mac

WORKSHEET

1. Do you believe you can hit?

2. Do you love the game of baseball?

3. How's your vision? Do you need an eye exam?

4. Do you know when and where you are looking?

5. Do you understand your contact points?

6. What is your approach vs. a pitcher you've never seen before?

7. How's your mental game?

8. Can you feel yourself becoming a fearless hitter?

9. Are you learning how to study pitchers?

10. What drills are you doing to improve your vision?

11. Are you working on your 2 strike approach to become dangerous?

12. Can you classify pitchers?

13. Can you hear the music to determine the pitcher's delivery tempo?

14. Can you identify the pitcher's arm slot?

15. Are you learning to determine a pitcher's pitches and out pitch?

16. Are you working on being a well rounded baseball player?

17. Are you accurately and honestly evaluating yourself?

18. Do you have some mental skills?

19. What tools do you have in your mental toolbox?

20. What did you learn from the Long Beach State players?

21. What did you learn from the pro players before they were professionals?

22. Do you have actions that prove you love baseball?

23. Have you taken ownership of your career?

24. What areas in your life are you learning to win?

25. Can you situational hit?

26. What's your favorite situation? Why?

27. Are you having fun? Did I say this enough to let you know it's important? Did I just see you smile?

28. What swing goal are you working on currently? Vision, Rhythm and timing, balance, strength or bat path and bat speed? Why?

29. Can you dance with the pitcher?

30. Can you get into a good position to hit consistently on time?

30. Are you taking your career seriously and making swing coaches earn your trust?

RESOURCES

- Steve Springer: Qualityatbats.com
- H.A. Dorfman/ Karl Kuehl book: The Mental Game of Baseball: A Guide to Peak Performance
- Dean Karnazes: ultramarathonman.com
- Ken Ravizza books: Heads up Baseball, Heads up Baseball 2.0
- Karl Kuehl/ John Kuehl/ Casey Tefertiller book: Mental Toughness, - Baseball's Winning Edge
- Tim S. Grover/ Shari Wenk book: Relentless: From Good to Great to Unstoppable
- Nick Saban/Brian Curtis book: How Good Do You Want to Be? A Champion's Tips on How to Lead and Succeed at Work and in Life
- Richard Machowicz book: Unleashing the Warrior Within
- Mike Cernovich book: Gorilla Mindset
- Jocko Willink book: Extreme Ownership: How U.S. Navy Seals Lead and Win
- Mike Krzyzewski/ Donald T. Phillips/ Grant Hill book: Leading With the Heart
- baseballcube.com
- baseball-refrence.com
- 643charts.com

ABOUT THE AUTHOR

Tim McDonnell has an extensive career in baseball as a player, college coach and major league baseball scout. He's responsible for signing several major leaguers including two MLB MVPs: Giancarlo Stanton and Christian Yelich. Prior, he was the college hitting coach for Evan Longoria and Troy Tulowitzki among others. Tim provides valuable insight to help hitters develop their own complete hitting plan while maximizing their vision, mental skills, swing mechanics and more. Discover common traits of the best hitters in the world and find ways to make them your own. Read stories of players he coached and scouted before they were major leaguers and learn from them. Tim makes it clear this book isn't about him, but rather how fortunate he's been to learn from elite coaches and players he's had the privilege of working with. His goal is to share that information so players can conquer their fears by eliminating self-doubt, reignite their love of hitting, never give up and become Fearless Hitters.

"The potential for fear to dominate our mind starts the first day of playing baseball and doesn't go away until the very last. It begins with our own fears of being hit by the ball, striking out or making mistakes. Then quickly moves to outside sources pushing fear; your swing isn't perfect, you're not getting the right information, you have to do this or listen to that. The noise is overwhelming for parents and players, but it doesn't have to be. The good news is you CAN overcome fear, reignite your love of hitting and the game and get back to having fun while improving each and every day." Tim

Made in the USA
Columbia, SC
08 September 2023

22617300R00102